GOOD FRIDAY year 2633
THE END
OF WORLD
AS HIDDEN IN THE Bible

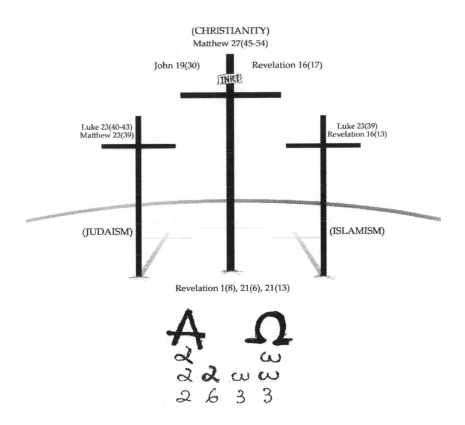

(CHRISTIANITY)
Matthew 27(45-54)

John 19(30)   Revelation 16(17)

INRI

Luke 23(40-43)   Luke 23(39)
Matthew 23(39)   Revelation 16(13)

(JUDAISM)   (ISLAMISM)

Revelation 1(8), 21(6), 21(13)

ANTHONY LENH DINH NGO

authorHOUSE®

AuthorHouse™
1663 Liberty Drive
Bloomington, IN 47403
www.authorhouse.com
Phone: 1-800-839-8640

Published by AuthorHouse   10/18/2012

ISBN: 978-1-4772-4937-6 (sc)
ISBN: 978-1-4772-4938-3 (e)

Library of Congress Control Number: 2012913136

THE FIRST WORDS

This is not my own prophecy. It is an answer which is found in the Book of the prophet Ezekiel, the Book of the prophet Daniel, the Revelation of Saint John, the Words of Jesus Christ, and the Death of the Lord Jesus on the Golgotha Hill.

Anthony Lenh Dinh Ngo
October 28, 2010

CONTENTS

CHAPTER 1

THE OPENING

Recently, many people have been discussing about the END DAY. Months before the year 2000, T.V., the media spoke about computers crashing and therefore, anything run by computer would shut down causing accidents, banks losing account information, stock market crashing, etc. Also, some prophets said that the world will end at year 2000. People became nervous and scared so they stocked up on food, water, medicine . . . However, the year 2000 came with no accident.

Now, the focus is on year 2012. What is it this time? Some scientists predict that on December 21th, 2012, the sun will move to the center of our galaxy, which is called a "Galactic Alignment". When this occur, it is suppose to cause a number of disasters, such as floods, earthquakes, tsunamis, etc. The prophet Nostradamus had written about this incident. The Mayan's also predicted that in the year 2012 the sun would move to the center of the galaxy, and the Mayan calender ends with 2012. Therefore, many people believe that on December 21th, 2012 the world will be ended. Could it be possible?

For over a thousand years, people have been discussing about the END DAY, they had picked many END dates, but so far they were all wrong. Jesus told his disciples and the Jews very clearly that the END DAY must be occurred. He gave many disasters and terrible warning signs before and on the END DAY. However, He did not provide an exact date: "But of that day and hour no one know, neither the angels of heaven, nor the Son, but the Father alone". Matthew 24(36).

Only God, the Father know the END DAY; however God did reveal to prophet Ezekiel and prophet Daniel in the Old Testament, and the image of the Death of Jesus, the Revelation of St. John in the New Testament about the END DAY. In this book, little by little we will discuss more about them.

But first, we need to know who is God? How are mankind created? And why God would want to destroyed the whole world?

Who is GOD?

Most religion define God as the one who creates the universe and mankind. However, some scientists believe that the universe was formed by itself and processed by law of gravity forces, no necessary has God. Recently, scientists have discovered the universe is still expanding. Therefore, they agree on the "big bang" theory where the universe was created at one extremely small point and a "big bang" expanded rapidly until now. But did this by itself or by God?

Most religions believe every person has soul, and when our bodies die, our souls will live in another world. But some scientists believe that God and our souls are figment in our heads. I believe God created the brain like a computer and the soul is like a computer program. The program runs the computer like the soul controls the mind. The computer connects to the internet center like the soul connects to God. So, praying to God is like downloading and Satan is like a virus. We suffer through sinful acts and the environment just like the virus gets into the program to destroy the computer. As the hardware and memory in a computer needs to be cleaned and updated in order to allow the software to run more effectively, people use yoga, therapy, and/or medicine to clear their minds. Other use faith in God to help them have a peace of mind like updating a computer program. When our bodies die, our souls will go to God or Satan, our knowledge will remain if it is written in the book or something else. Likewise, when the power off, the computer will stop running, but the information is saved in the disks or return to the internet center.

Who is God? Our ancestor believed in God that why we have many religions. Some scientists who doubt the existence of God theorize that, thousands of years ago, the "Ancient UFO" from other planet came to live with mankind and then our ancestors worshiped them like God. If that was true then all religions are fooling! Scientists have found the remain of some cities thousands of years old that highly constructed so they concluded that aliens must have been responsible for the knowledge to construct these cities. As a result, God does not exist.

In fact, the universe is enormous. Yes, there might be life on other planets, but that doesn't mean God does not exist. Rather, God created them as well. The existence of aliens does not weaken the existence of God, but strength it.

The creation story in the book of Genesis6(1-4) hint at the existence of aliens:" When men began to multiply on earth and daughters were born to them, the sons of heaven saw how beautiful the daughters of man were, and so they took for their wives as many of them as they chose. Then the Lord said: 'My Spirit shall not remain in man forever, since he but flesh. His day shall comprise one hundred and twenty years.'

At that time the Nephilim appeared on earth (as well as later), after the sons of heaven had intercourse with the daughters of man, who bore them sons. They were the heroes of old, the men of renown."

This was happened right before "The Great Flood", the time that God was very disappointed with mankind:

Genesis 6(5-7): "When the Lord saw how great was man's wickedness on earth, and how no desire that his heart conceived was ever anything but evil, He regretted that He had made man on earth, and His heart was grieved.

So the Lord said:' I will wipe out from the earth the men whom I had created, and not only the men, but also the beasts and creeping things and the birds of the air for I am sorry that I made them.' But Noah found favor with the Lord."

After "The Great Flood", everyone was died except Noah' family.

Is there God? Most people believe in God: God is invisible, the most perfect, goodness and powerful one; God created Heaven, Hell, and our Natural Universe. Our experiences in this world are that, everything have to be made by someone or some factories, and the Spirit is invisible, powerful over mankind. We see all incredible things surround us, the big things far away like stars, planets or small things close to us like our bodies. God must be exist. But where is God come from? We can not answer because our brains are too small, our knowledge are too little compare to God; just like we can understand animals more than they can understand us.

HOW WAS MANKIND CREATED?

In the Bible, the book of Genesis contains the story of creation where God made the universe, water, plants, and animals. Finally, God made the first man, Adam, by using mud and had the Spirit flow in him. God let Adam live in the garden of Eden where Adam could eat any fruit in the garden except the tree of knowledge in the middle of the garden. Genesis 1(16-17):

"From that tree you shall not eat; the moment you eat from it you are surely doomed to die." And when Adam slept deeply, God took one of his ribs to make a woman named Eve. Eventually, Eve listened to the serpent Satan and ate the fruit from the forbidden tree and gave it to Adam, who also ate it. When God called, they knew their sin and hid in the trees. God drove them out of the garden. God said to the serpent:

> "I will put enmity between you and the woman,
> and between your offspring and hers.
> He will strike at your head,
> while you strike at his heal"
>
> Genesis 3(15)

From that time on, man has had to work hard to survive.

Scientists believe in the theory of evolution where all living things on earth change over time to adapt to their environment. Although the creation story in the Bible is different with the theory of evolution, but over few thousand years ago, our ancestors understood better in the story of Bible than the scientific. The story in Genesis teach us that God created all things and that good and evil exist side by side among us, and it is up to each of us to choose which we will follow.

CHAPTER 2

HOW DO PHILOSOPHERS THINK ABOUT GOD?

2.1   Philosophers and philosophy.

Many people have thoughts, ideas for their lives and for societies, question about who creates the universe, what will be happened to us after our death ... Some of them are famous and known in the world as philosophers and their ideas called philosophy; most early philosophers from Ancient Greece:

- Thales: Perhaps he was considered as the first philosopher who said that, all things are made out of water, everything that exists is really water in more or less complicated form.
- Anaximander: The world is made of substance called apeion, which produces the basic element of earth, air, water and fire.
- Anaximenes: The world is made of fire.
- Pythagoras: A famous mathematician said that the world is an embodiment of numbers.

Philosophy consists all kinks of thinking: social science, natural science, math, religion . . . There are three main branches of philosophy: ontology(being), epistemology(knowing), and ethics(acting).

BEING (Ontology)

Many philosophers use idea about "Being" to prove existence of God. They argue that the universe is very organize and support life so God must have planned it. Therefore, the world exists, so God must exists.

KNOWING (Epistemology)

Epistemology is the study of knowledge, what we can know and how we know it.

- Rene Descartes: The fact that he could think told him for certain that he existed. His famous words: "I think therefore I am". He viewed that the world is made of material and spiritual aspects called "Dualism". Spiritual part of reality is confined to God and the human mind; the remain of reality is physical. Many philosophers agree this idea. The mind is capable of knowing things even without experiences, they call this is "Rationalism".
- Baruch Spinoza: Matter itself could think, even all rocks, trees, mountain, rivers . . . , they are alive and capable of knowing, and all reality itself is God. God and Nature are two sides of the same coin. This view called "Vitalism".
- Francis Bacon, John Lock: The best way to certain of something is to test it through your actual experience. This base for science called "Empiricism".
- Immanuel Kant: He brought "Rationalism" and "Empiricism" together to make a different way of thinking called "Idealism".
- Karl Marx: Knowledge is limited and structured by the way we see to our material needs. Karl Marx called this structure of knowledge is "Ideology".

The different of Descartes and Marx is that: Descartes is thinking about knowing from inside the mind, asking what the mind can do entirely on its own; Marx is thinking about knowing from outside society, ask how economic form shape the way people think.

"Empiricism" and "Ideology" don't believe in spiritual reality and God.

Philosophers use three techniques of logic for acquiring and testing knowledge: deduction, induction and dialectic.

a) Deduction: Use two premises have fact true, we can deduct for certain conclusion. Here is Aristotle's syllogism about Socrates:

   _ All men are mortal.
   _ Socrates is man.
   _ Socrates is mortal.

b) Induction: Use two premises in fact true to get a conclusion but not certain:

_ One deer has yellow color.

_ Many deers have yellow color.

_ Probably color of all deers are yellow.

c) Dialectic: Dialectic means discussion in Greek word. Socrates believed that learning how little we know for certain was the best way to gain knowledge. Socrates tested ideas logically by moving back and forth between ideas helped him to see how accurate they were. This back and forth called "dialectic". This method is very useful, can apply for many topics of political, religion, economic, society . . .

Human being continue to figure out the ways of thinking and learning, try to gain more knowledge. Knowledge of individual is a small part of knowledge of whole world. Knowledge of whole world is too small comparing with knowledge of God. Philo, a Jewish philosopher said:

"People's mind are model after God's mind, so we can understand God through reason_to a point_ but material thing limit people's ability to reason, therefore, we need faith to connect with God". Also Leibniz said: "People have finite mind but God has infinite mind".

ACTING (Ethics)

Ethics include all ideas about acting of individual and society, relate between people and with God. Acting has been changing by history and by area where people live. People of the East more "collectivistic" but Westerners tend to be more "individualistic". In the West, religion, philosophy, science, capitalism and democracy have all promoted Individualism.

a) Eastern philosophy:
 • Confucius (551BC_479BC): A Chinese philosopher, believed that people should act in harmony with society, from farmer to ruler, each person has a role in society, some roles more important than other, respect each other from individual role in a family to outside society by "Li"(behaving with courtesy and ceremoniousness) all work together to have peace and happiness.

- Lao_tzu: A Chinese philosopher, he lived around same time with Confucius. Different idea with Confucius, Lao_tzu taught that, people need harmony with nature rather than with society. Nature itself keep changing in circle from "yin" to "yang", so do people from "happy" to "suffer", therefore, we don't have to worry, live in happiness in every circumstance.

b) Indian philosophy:
- Hindu: from ancient writing as known as the "Vedas". The "Vedas" gives a number of rules for people and Hindu Gods should live, they call dharma, the dharma is determined by your caste, your occupation . . . By live right with your dharma you will get better from cycles of karma after you die and reincarnate in a new life with richer and power instead of poor or become insects, animals . . .
- Buddha: Buddha means "Awakened One", the name was given to Siddhartha Gautama(563BC_483BC). His belief similar like Hindu but he rejected caste system. His ideas that all lives are suffering, even Gods. We are all tied to suffering by our desire. So, we need transcend suffering by eliminating selfish desire with Eight fold paths:
  - _ Right seeing.
  - _ Right thinking.
  - _ Right speaking.
  - _ Right acting.
  - _ Right lifestyle.
  - _ Right effort.
  - _ Right mindset.
  - _ Right mediating.

- Mohandas "Mahatma" Gandhi(1896_1948): He practiced Hindu by emphasized self denial, he also taught the principle of ahimsa non-violence toward all ling things. With this idea, he took back independent for India from Great Britain.

c) Middle Eastern religious philosophy: Three big religions in Middle East, Judaism, Christianity and Islamism had same an ancestor Abraham. About 4,000 years ago, Abraham who was chosen by God, and was led to the promise land; now become Israel country with Jewish people, and their religion: Judaism. From Jewish people, 2,000 years ago, Jesus as a Son of God came to earth to save our sins: Christianity. After Jesus 610 years(610AD), Muhammad claimed as a God's last prophet and their religion: Islamism. Muhammad was also a descendent of Abraham with second wife.

All three religions believe in one God, God of Abraham, God created Heaven, Hell, earth and universe. God is powerful and good. Evil is bad and try to tempt human being to against God. They all believe life after death, happiness or suffering after death depends on how we live right now in this world.

d) Western philosophy:
  * Socrates (469BC_399BC): He gave a famous method "dialectic", keep ask question and debate back and forth we will find the truth ideas and also able to poke holes in other people ideas. He did not believe the God of ancient Greek and causing a threat to society at his time, he chose to die rather than renounce his beliefs by drink poison "hemlock".
  * Plato (428BC_347BC): He was a student of Socrates, he believed that philosophers should be kings. A peaceful society has to have three classes of people: rulers, soldiers and traders. Philosophers are rulers and soldiers help rulers to keep the traders in line.
  * Aristotle (384BC_322BC): He was a student of Plato, He said that, too little or too much of anything could be bad. People shouldn't do anything excess in their lives, if they want happiness. That is called Aristotle's "golden means".
  * Zeno (490BC_425BC): Zeno and others like Seneca, Epictetus, Marcus Aurelius in Rome, they believed that good or bad things happen to you are out of your control. So, who care, it doesn't matter, don't worry about that, you need to focus to make your life happier. You just do what need to do, this is called "Stoicism".
  * Epicurus (341BC_270BC): His philosophy was called "Epicureans". Life is happy, so every thing make your life happy are good: eating, drinking, sex or . . . He believes our souls will dissolve to atom after we die, so don't worry, just enjoy this life. Epicurus advised avoid getting married and politics because these thing make your mind unpeaceful.

* Pyrrho (365BC_270BC): He taught that, we can not know the truth, all ideas that may or may not be true. People can agree or disagree about one idea depend on their senses.
* Francis Bacon (1561_1626): People have four mistaken ideas, he called "idols of the mind":
  _ Idols of the tribe: Mistakes caused by human nature. We live same tribe, perceptions and emotions are inherently unreliable.
  _ Idols of the cave: Mistakes caused by tendencies of individual. We have own way of understand like to live in our own "cave".
  _ Idols of the market place: Mistakes caused by convention. People often agree on thing that not base on the truth, instead "buy and sell" ideas by socially valuable.
  _ Idols of the theater: Mistakes caused by philosophical authorities. Some philosophers just want to show off their wisdom even they don't know they talking about.

These idols confuse people make them thinking more wrong than right. So, people need to clean up their mind to find the truth. Bacon suggest focus to nature by make sure our ideas logically, and test their accuracy by performing experiment of science. He said: "If a man begins with certainties, he will end in doubts, but if he will be content to begin with doubts, he shall end in certainties".

* Rene Descartes (1591_1650): He disagreed with Bacon who just believe in pure physical science. We need also the mind which is not simply made of material matter, it is also made up of spirit.
* Thomas Hobbes (1588_1679): He was a friend of Bacon, argued that, people ought to obey the king even if he is a tyrant. We need strong ruler to keep people out of killing and stealing from each other. "The condition of man is a condition of war of everyone against everyone". Without government we would live in "the state of nature", a dog_eat_dog world with no peace.
* Issac Newton (1642_1727): He was one of early scientist who applied mathematics to physical things. Newton developed a famous formula for all moving things:

Force = motion x acceleration

He also figured out formula for describing the force of gravity. He found that the beam of light can be separated by a prism in to colors of the spectrum: red, orange, yellow, green, blue, indigo and violet. This means that color is result of light that bounces off materials; each material reflects certain color of light.

Issac Newton gave the world a new law of physic, open a new way for science.

* John Lock (1632_1704): People have the nature right to make free choices, to live without being injured by other; they have the right to work and own property. Lock wanted to separate God and government, against the idea of many people in that time: "The divine right of king".

* Charles Louis (Baron de Montesquieu), (1689_1755): His ideas about "the separation of power" in government. This later was written into the U.S. Constitution and the Constitution of the French Republic.

* John Stuart Mill (1806_1873): He believed that all things have causes and human being have free will. His "utilitarianism" is view that any action is good if it leads to human happiness, and bad if it stands in the way of happiness. The more freedom people have, the happier they will be.

* Karl Marx (1818_1883): The way people live determined by the "relation of production". Many Communist countries have applied Marx's ideas like Soviet Union, China, Vietnam, Cuba, North Korea, but it has not worked as Marx's thought. The result is government getting too much power to control people; people lost all their freedom, and the production is slow down, economic goes to corruption. Communist party members gain more benefit but majority people are suffer.

* Nietzsche (1844_1900): Individual is special important, capable of developing into power like "superman". Opposite with "superman" is "the herd": All those average people who like to stick together and think, act alike. They feel safe that way, but "the herd" prevents people from creating new ways of thinking and acting. You should live for yourself and disregard feeling of "the herd". Good and Evil are just "heard like" ideas that lead to a safe and boring existence; we need to look "beyond good and evil" if we want to realize our potential for living.

* New Ages: New Ages have been very popular in the 1980 and still strong today. They reject most tradition Western thinking and embraces just about everything else. They believe that we all have the power to transform the world. We can in control and make the world the way we want it to be when we learn to develop our mental power: another word, we can be Gods.

They use the famous formula of Einstein to verify their ideas:

$$E = mc^2$$
E : Energy
m: Mass (quantity of matter)
c : Speed of light

Every matter including people are made up of energy in one state or another. So, our bodies are tremendous of energy that we are all united to the Cosmos.

They search for a "global oneness" by combination all religions in the world together. They use Taoism, Buddhism and Hinduism like meditation, yoga, the I ching to develop power of our bodies, and make a clean planet, a good place for living.

In short, New Ages search for new ways to think and live common for all philosophy in a clean planet.

2.2   Philosophers verify God.

Many philosophers believe in God but see God with many different ways, different images. Also, some don't believe in God at all. Following are several examples:

a) Philosophers believe in God:

* Socrates (469BC_399BC) and his student Plato (428BC_347BC): Believed God created the universe from his likeness. They also believed in immortality of souls.

* Aristotle (384BC_322BC): He was student of Plato, said that God is Unmoved Mover, the casual source of our world not personally related to it and carry nothing for us or for our worship. Aristotle didn't believe in an after life or immortality of the soul; all living things like plants, animals, humans have souls but they die with bodies, so we rather enjoy our lives while it last.

* Philo (30BC_45AD): The ideal good and God is the same thing.
* Saint Augustine (354_430): People can only get close to God without actually dying and go to heaven. If we really want to experience God, we have to wait until our lives end, at that time our souls will be not tied down to physical reality.
* Saint Anselm (1033_1109): If something are perfect, it must be exist, since non_existence is a sign of imperfection. The most perfect thing we can think of is God. Because God is perfect, he must be exist.
* Saint Thomas Aquinas (1225_1274): Five ways to prove existence of God:

  _ Motion: Through sense experience, we encounter things being "moved" to change "from potentiality to actuality". Therefore it is necessary to arrive at a first mover moved by no other; and this everyone understand to be God.

  _ Efficient cause: We experience and come to understand "an order of efficient cause". Therefore, It is necessary to admit a first efficient cause to which everyone give the name of God.

  _ Possibility and necessity: Objects of our experience that continuity exist. Not all being are merely possible but there must exist something the existence of which is necessary. That necessary being either derives its necessity from another or it does not. If it does, that process of derivation can not go on but admit the existence of some being having itself, its own necessity and not receiving its from another. This all men speak out as God.

  _ Quality: We experience objects are present of quality "some more and some less good, true, noble, and the like". "The maximum in any genus is the cause of all in that genus". There must also be something which is to all being the cause of being goodness and over other perfection, and this we called God.

  _ Governance of the world: The organize and moving of universe must be "directed by some being endowed with knowledge and intelligent". "Therefore some intelligent being exist by whom all natural things are directed to their end; and this being we call God".

* Rene Descartes (1591_1650): A spiritual portion of our mind allows us to understand perceptions that are converted to us physically by our senses, that spiritual portion of reality was confined to God.
* Baruch Spinoza (1632_1677): Reality itself is God. God and Nature are two sides of the same coin.
* Leibniz (1646_1716): People have finite mind, God has infinite mind.

b) Philosophers do not believe or have very little faith in God:
   - Francis Bacon (1561_1626): People have mistaken ideas "idols of the mind", they worship their false beliefs as if they are false gods. He believed that "the idols of the mind" had confused people, so we just throw all that away to focus just on nature.
   - Thomas Hobbes (1588_1679): The mind is completely physical, It is made up of material matter, there is nothing spiritual or magical about it.
   - Karl Marx (1818_1883): The way people live is determined by the "relation of production". Religion, philosophy, and popular belief reflect a society's power structure and at the same time compel people to fit in with that structure.
   - Nietzche (1844_1900): You should live for yourself, the thing make you happy are not determined by what other people think but by you. Good and evil are just "herd like" ideas that lead to a safe, quiet, and boring existence.
   - Stephen Hawking (1942_): He is a famous English physical scientist, published the book "The Grand Design" on year 2010 that: "Science can explain the universe origin without invoking God". "In the end, science will win".

As we know, philosophers have many different view about God. When we see the beauty and wonder of nature, we can feel God; just like the artist draws pictures, he put his thoughts in them, and then people who see the pictures, they might feel the artist's spirit. It is very difficult to very God, although many philosophers have been tried this, but to a point, we still need faith. One thing certain is that, we can never discover everything of the wonder of the universe which some scientists say that it formed by itself not by God! Our knowledge is very small comparing with the knowledge of God; just like animals and us, we can know much about them, but they understand us very limited.

Human being is very complex, we are bouncing in the material world and between good and evil, and we also have free will to think, to say, to act.

CHAPTER 3

THE MAINLY RELIGIONS IN THE WORLD

There are many religions in the world, most religions worship God as Creator, very powerful, goodness and invisible; but some religions worship human being like ancestors, heroes, animals . . . Most people's religion get chosen by family affiliation. That is, whatever religion they grew up with is usually the religion they followed. Some are forced into their religions by the government of which ever country they live in. Sometimes, the religion itself uses the force of violence to prevent followers from leaving. Religion is a highly sensitive, and sometimes a highly volatile topic that has been the basis for much conflict, even wars. The following will outline the most popular of the world's religions: Hinduism, Buddhism, Judaism, Christianity, Islamism.

3.1   Hinduism: (900 million followers)

Perhaps, the oldest religion in the world is Hinduism. No one know exactly when it was formed and who was its founder. It may have been formed over 5000 years ago, but it was written down about 1000 years before Christ (1000B.C.). Hinduism believe in many Gods, such as the sun, moon, lightning, etc, and each God has a mystical story. Some Gods can take on animal form, such as elephants, cows, birds, snakes, etc. Hinduism believe in Samsara, which is the cycle of birth, life, and rebirth. When the cycle ends, they will be with Gods in Nirvana or Samadi. They also believe in Karma: every action has a cause and effect. Yoga is highly used as a way to purify the mind and body in order to reach Samadi.

3.2   Buddhism: (376 millions followers)

Siddhartha Gautama, also known as the Buddha (Awaken One), was founder of Buddhism. He was born in Lumbini around the year 563 B.C. And raised in Kapilavastu, which is the modern day Nepal. He was a prince who was married and had a son. When he was twenty—nine years old, he saw the suffering of mankind, he left the kingdom and his family to find the spirit of life. He practiced fast and meditation; one time he fast breath-holding and exposure to pain, he almost stared himself into death. When he was thirty-five years old, he often sit under Bohi tree to fast. He died at the age of eighty (about 483 B.C.) in Kushinagar, India. Some people believe he died from eating a poisoned mushroom soup by a blacksmith named Cunda.

There are two branches of Buddhism: Theravada and Mahayama. Like Hinduism, Buddhism believe in Karma and (cause and effect) and Samsara(cycle of suffering and rebirth). According to Theravada, there are five realms of rebirth or six according other schools:

*   Naraka beings: Those souls who live in one of many Naraka (Hells).
*   Preta: The souls live with human like hungry ghost.
*   Animals: The souls live with human but become animals.
*   Human being: Rebirth to human being, at this level, if good enough next life has a chance to get in Nirvana; if not, next life will be down to some levels.

    Asuras: Become demons, titans.
*   Devas include Brahmas: Gods, angels, spirits.

Special rebirth:

_   Higher heavens like Suddhavasa worlds (Pure Abodes) only by skilled Buddhist practictioners as Anaga mis (non-returners).

_   Rebirth in the Arupadhatu (formless realms, for people who can meditate on the Arupajhanas).

Buddhism also practice yoga, meditation to purify the mind and body. Many people believe that Buddhism come from Hinduism, but Buddhism don't teach about Gods, no mention Gods in Buddhism.

3.3 Judaism: (14 million followers)

Judaism originated from Israel, a country in the Middle East. This religion was not founded by mankind looking for God, but God reached down to mankind. About the year 1921B.C., God appeared to Abram saying: "Go forth from land of your kinsfolk and from your father's house to land that I will show you. I will make you a great nation, and I will bless you; I will make your name great so that you will be a blessing. I will bless those who bless you and curse who curse you. All the communities of the earth shall find blessing in you." Genesis 12(1-3). Abram led his wife and some relatives from the land of his father, which is modern day Turkey, to the direction that God had showed him, which is modern day Israel.

God changed his name from Abram to Abraham. God protected and blessed Abraham and his offspring in Israel with an up and down history. God has appeared to these "chosen people" directly to their leaders or through the mouth of prophets. History of Israel was written down in books we now call the Bible.

From one Abraham, one country Israel, one tribe Judea, one line of king David, God sent his Son to the world: that is Christianity.

3.4 Christianity: (2.1 billion followers)

Christianity believe in Jesus Christ, Son of God, comes to the world to save mankind from their sins. Christianity includes: Orthodox, Catholic, Protestant, Non-trinitarian . . .

The following is from the Gospel of Luke 1(26-38):

" . . . , the angel Gabriel was sent from God to a town of Galilee called Nazareth to a virgin betrothed to a man name Joseph, of house of David, and the virgin's name was Mary. And coming to her, he said, 'Hail, favored one! The Lord is with you.' But she was greatly troubled at what was said and pondered what sort of greeting this might be. Then the angel said to her 'Do not be afraid Mary, for you have found favor with God. 'Behold, you will conceive in your womb and bear a son, and you shall name him Jesus. He will be great and will be called Son of the Most High and the Lord God will give him the throne of David his father, and he will rule over the house of Jacob forever, and his kingdom there will be no end.' But Mary said to the angel: 'How can this be, since I have no relations with a man?' And the angel said to her in reply, 'The Holy Spirit will come upon you, and the power of the Most

High will over shadow you. Therefore the child to be born will be called holy, the Son of God. And behold, Elizabeth, your relative, has also conceived a son in her old age, and this is the sixth month for her who was called barren, for nothing will be impossible for God.' Mary said, 'Behold, I am the handmaid of the Lord. May it be done to me according to your words.'" Then the angel depart from her.

Luke 2(1-14): In those days a decree went out from Caesar Augustus that the whole world should be enrolled. This was the first enrollment, when Quirius was governor of Syria. So all went to be enrolled, each to his own town. And Joseph too went up from Galilee from the town of Nazareth to Judea, to the city of David that is called Bethlehem, because he was of house and family of David, to be enrolled with Mary, his betrothed, who was with child. While they were there, the time came for her to have her child, and she gave birth to her first born son. She wrapped him in swaddling clothes and laid him in a manger, because there was no room for them in the inn.

Now there was shepherds in that region living in the field and keeping the night watch over their flock. The angel of the Lord appeared to them, and the glory of the Lord shone around them, then they were struck with fear. The angel said to them, "Do not be afraid; for behold, I proclaim to you good news of great joy that will be for all the people. For today in the city of David a savior has been born for you who is Messiah and Lord. And this will be a sign for you: you will find an infant wrapped in swaddling clothes and lying in a manger". And suddenly there was a multitude of the heavenly host with the angel, praising God and saying: "Glory to God in the highest and on earth peace to those on whom his favor rest".

Jesus was born in Bethlehem of Judea and lived in Nazareth of Galilee. He had no wife. He began his ministry when he was thirty years old. He called twelve disciples, all were fisherman except Matthew was a tax collector. After three years of teaching and making a lots of miracles, Jesus was crucified by Pharisees (leaders of Judaism) and the soldiers of Roman Empire year 33A.D. Three days after his death, he rose up, appeared many times to disciples, comforted and sent them to teach the Good News for the whole world. He stayed on earth forty days before he went up to heaven in front of his disciples and the crowd.

The Christian Bible has two parts: The Old Testament and the New Testament. The Old Testament includes the story of Creation, the history of the Jewish people from Abraham to Jesus, and the books of a number of prophets. In this book we will discuss the book of prophet Ezekiel and the book of prophet Daniel concerning the END DAY, or the end of humanity as we know it. The New Testament includes the four Gospels who all wrote about the life of Jesus, his ministry, his teaching, his miracles, his death, and his resurrection; the Act of the Apostles contains the writing about the activity of the apostles in the formation of Christianity, their arrest, and their deaths; the letters of apostles to Christian Communities, the most of Saint Paul; The Book of Revelation of St. John contains his prophesies about the END DAY and will also be discussed in this book.

We can say that Christianity comes from Judaism; however, most Jews do not believe in Jesus even though the birth of Jesus fulfilled many of the prophecies that the Savior will come from the House of David and born by a virgin. The Jewish people had been waiting for a Savior to take Israel back from the Roman Empire. However, Jesus did not profess himself to be a leader that would give back the "promise land" to the Jews. Rather only proclaimed himself to be the Son of God, sent to save mankind from their sins.

3.5   Islamism: (1.5 billion followers)

Islamism was founded by the prophet Muhammad in the year 610 A.D. Muhammad was born in Mecca or modern day Saudi Arabia on April 20, 570 A.D. His father died shortly after he was born and his mother died when he was six years old. He lived with his grandfather, but after his grandfather died he lived with his uncle, Aba Talib. He followed his uncle from town to town like a merchant. When he was twenty-five years old, he married a forty year old widow named Khadija bint Khuwaylid who was a rich merchant. She was very smart. It is possible that without her, Muhammad may not become a prophet of Islam. Later, Muhammad had many wives, around thirteen women. Khadija gave Muhammad four daughters: Ruquayyah bint Muhammad, Umm Kulthum bint Muhammad, Zainab bint Muhammad, Fatimah Zahra bint Muhammad and two sons: Abd-Allah ibn Muhammmad, Qasim ibn Muhammad.

Two sons both died in childhood. All her children died before Muhammad except two daughters: Fatimah and Zainab. Shi'a scholars contend that Fatimah was Muhammad only daughter. Muhammad's descendents through Fatimah are known as "sharifs, sayeds or sayyids". These are honorific titles in Arabic, "sharif" meaning "noble" and "sayed" or "sayyid" meaning "Lord" or "Sir". As Muhammad's only descendents, they are respected by both Sunni and Shi'a, the two branches of Islamism.

These are wives of Muhammad:
_ Khadijah bint Khuwaylid
_ Sawda bint Zam'a
_ Aisha bint Abi Bakr
_ Hafsa bint Umar
_ Zaynab bint Khuzayma
_ Hind bint Abi Umayya
_ Zaynab bint Jahsh
_ Juwayriya bint al-Harith
. _ Ramlah bint Abi Sufyan
_ Rayhana bint Zayd
_ Safiyya bint Huyayy
_ Maymuna bint al-Harith
_ Maria al-Qibtiyya.

Maria al-Qibtiyya bore Muhammad a son named Ibrahim ibn Muhammad, but the child died when he was two years old. The remain had no children with Muhammad.

The wife who Muhammad loved the best was Aisha, he married her when she was nine years old and him fifty three years old. And another beautiful wife was Zaynab bint Jahsh who had been married to Zay, an adopted son of Muhammad.

When Muhammad was forty years old (610 A.D.), he went into a cave in Hira or modern day Saudi Arabia to pray and an angel sent from Allah (God) appeared to him. Ibn Sad records, an angel named "Seraphel" originally visited Muhammad and was replaced by "Gabriel" years later. Muhammad said: "The angel caught me (forcefully) and pressed me so hard that I could not bear it anymore. He then released me and asked me to read, and I replied, 'I do not now how to read (or what shall I read?).' Thereupon he caught me for the third time and pressed me and then released me and said: 'Read! In the Name of you Lord, who has created man from a clot. Read! and your Lord is most generous . . . [unto] . . . that which he knew not.'" (V.96:5)^21

Muhammad returned to Khadija (his wife) in tremendous distress. According Aisha, another wife: "Then Allah's messenger returned with that (the Revelation and his heart severely beating; and the muscles between his neck and shoulder were trembling till he came upon Khadija) and said: 'cover me.'" They cover him, till his fear was over, and after that he said: "O, Khadija what is wrong with me? I was afraid that something bad might happen to me."

Then he told her all that had happened. And he repeated to her his initial fear: "Woe is me poet or possessed?" He meant poet in the sense of one who received ecstatic, and possibly demonic visions.

Khadija was more confident than Muhammad. She went to see Waragua and told him Muhammad's story at the cave in Hira. Waragua explained to Khadija that the Gabriel angel who came to Moses now appeared to Muhammad so he must be a prophet of his people. Khadija told Muhammad what Aragua had said lessening Muhammad's anxiety. After that, he often went to the cave in Hira and the angel taught him more. And the cave in Hira became a Holy place for Islam. Muhammad's first followers were his wife Khadija and his uncle, Abu Talib. Later, he formed an army and occupied the surrounding area and created Islam. He died in the year 632 A.D., at sixty-two years old from illness. The illness may have come about from poisoned food he ate prepared for him by a Jewish woman named Zaynab bint al Hrith three years before at Khaybar. (The Truth about Muhammad by Robert Spencer).

The Qur'an is the Bible of Islam. It contains the revelations by the angel Gabriel revealed to Prophet Muhammad. Islamism believed in Abraham and the prophets of Judaism. Like Judaism, Islamism do not believe that Jesus is the Son of God. But unlike Judaism, Islamism believed Jesus was a prophet, and Muhammad to be the last prophet of God (Allah).

These above are five mainly religions of many religions in the world. Most believe in God, but by different ways. In order to find the true God, we need the freedom of religions, separate religions from politics, governments and the power of religion leaders who wants to control their followers.

CHAPTER 4

WHO ARE ANTI-CHRIST?

Satan and his offspring are the anti-Christ. Remember, God said to Satan in the garden Eden.

> "I will put enmity between you and the woman,
> and between your offspring and hers,
> He will strike at your head,
> while you strike at his heel."
>
> Genesis 3(15).

Therefore the battle between Jesus and Satan began from Jesus' birth until the END TIME. Satan had found many ways by use power of humankind to sabotage God's plan to save mankind by Jesus.

* One such even was after Jesus was born King Herod ordered a massacre of the infants in Bethlehem and its vicinity two years old and under. According to Matthew 2(13-5): The angel of the Lord appeared to Joseph in a dream and said: "Rise, take the child and his mother, flee to Egypt, and stay there till I tell you. Herod is going to search for the child to destroy him." Joseph rose and took the child and his mother by night and departed for Egypt. He stayed there until the death of Herod. This was what God had said through the prophet might be fulfilled, "'Out of Egypt I called my Son.'"

* Another incident was when Jesus was thirty years old. After Jesus was baptized by John the Baptist to prepare himself for his ministry, he went to the desert alone to pray and fast for forty days and forty nights. During this time of pray and fasting, Satan appeared and tempted him. Satan told Jesus that if Jesus followed him, everything in this world would belong to Jesus. Jesus replied to Satan: "Get away, Satan! It is written: 'The Lord your God, shall you worship and him alone shall you serve.'" Matthew 4(1-10).

4.1 Judaism Against Jesus:

* During the three years of Jesus' ministry, he performed many miracles and many Jewish people followed him. However, the Pharisees, the leaders of Judaism, were threatened by him. They were threatened by the number of people following him and angry at him for reprimanding them in public when their actions were counter to the teachings of Moses. Jesus command his disciples: "Beware of the leaven—that is, the hypocrisy—of the Pharisees.Matthew 23(1-39). Finally, they found only one sentence to crucified him: "He proclaim himself Son of God." Luke 12(1).

* After Jesus rose from death, some of the guards reported what had occurred on the mountain and that truly Jesus was the Son of God. But the chief priests, persuaded the guards that they must have been mistaken. "'While they were going, some of the guard went into the city and told the chief priests all that had happened. They assembled with the elders and took counsel; then they gave a large sum of money to the soldiers, telling them "You are to say, 'His disciples came by night and stole him while we were asleep.' And if this gets to the ears of the governor we will satisfy (him) and keep you out of trouble". The soldiers took the money and did as they were instructed. And this story has circulated amongst the Jews to this present day". Matthew 28(11-15).

* The Pharisees wanted to destroy Christianity right from the beginning of the Church. They and Roman Empire have pursued and killed many Christians. All disciples of Jesus were fishermen, except Matthew (tax collector), they were very low education, no weapon, only faith. However, Christians kept growing bigger. Many people converted to Christianity. One such person was St. Paul. He once lead the killing of early Christians, but later converted and became a great saint in Christianity. Besides physically killing Christians, the Pharisees attempted to destroy Christians' faith by spreading rumors such as Jesus did not rise from the dead, the person who was crucified was not Jesus, also the rumor that Mary Magdalene was Jesus' wife, etc.

Recently, many times at Easter season, the news broadcast on T. V. that some archeologists found a cave containing the supposed tombs of Jesus' family: Joseph, Mary, Jesus, Mary Magdalene. And some books from over thousand years have been found in some areas. These "findings" contained some information against the faith of Christianity. Is it possible that these had been planed by Pharisees and Roman Empire from thousands of years ago, and they now act as false evidence against Jesus and Christianity?

The Pharisees will fight against Jesus until the END DAY as Jesus said: "Jerusalem, Jerusalem, you who kill the prophets and stone those sent to you, how many times I yearned to gather your children together, as a hen gathers her young under her wings, but you were unwilling! Behold, your house will be abandoned, desolate. I tell you, you will not see me again until you say, 'Blessed is he who come in the name of the Lord.'" Matthew 23(37-39).

4.2   Islamism Against Jesus

Islam believe Jesus is a prophet, but do not believe what his teachings; the prophet of God always tell the truth. In the beginning, Muhammad destroyed many tribes belonging to Jews and Christians. The Jihad movement rose up and killed all nonbelievers to Islam. Islamism is similar to Judaism in that it rejects Jesus' work, the plan of God, although they worship God very much. God wants to save humankind from their sins by body and blood of Jesus. He accepts no more sacrificed animals but only Jesus, the "Lamb of God", as John Baptist said when he saw Jesus coming to him for the baptize: "'The next day he saw Jesus coming toward him and said: "Behold, the Lamb of God who takes away the sin of the world. He is the one of whom I said, 'A man is coming after me who ranks ahead of me because he exist before me.'" John 1(29-30).

4.3   Christianity Against Jesus

Christians believe in Jesus, but Christians rail against him in many ways, such as in their weakness of faith, their hypocrisy. There were twelve disciples of Jesus, but one, Judas, betrayed him. How many Judas' in over 2 billion Christians in the world right now?

4.4   The World Against Jesus

Money, power, sex . . . belong to this world. Jesus said: "No one can serve two masters. He will either hate one and despite the other. You can not serve God and mammon." Matthew 6(24). Mankind tend to shift to Bad than Good. The world either ignore Jesus or against his teaching.

CHAPTER 5

THE END DAY

Again, remember God's words to Satan serpent in the garden of Eden:

> "I will put enmity between you and the woman,
> and between your offspring and hers,
> He will strike at our head,
> while you strike at his heel."
>
> Genesis 3(15).

So, the END DAY will be finish the long war between Satan and Jesus that began at Jesus' birth. God gave Satan the power to persuade mankind to his side while Jesus is Son of God, although he has power even Satan has to knee down before him, but Jesus has to obey his Father's will. God is very fair in this war, so maybe that is why Jesus was unable to discover the date in which the world would end: "But of that day and hour, no one knows, neither the angels of heaven, nor the Son, but the Father alone." Matthew 24(36).

5.1 The END DAY according to Jesus.

A few days before Jesus was crucified, he told his disciples and the crowd about the END DAY. The Gospels of Matthew, Mark, Luke were all speaking of the END DAY except the gospel of John. However, the author of Revelations prophesied about the END DAY named John. There is no evidence to verify that these two books are by the same "John", but they were written around the same time.

*   The END DAY has to come as Jesus said: "Heaven and earth will pass away, but my words will not pass away." Matthew 24(35).

*   The signs of END DAY:

_ Matthew 24(15-21): "**When** you see the desolating abomination spoken of through **Daniel** the prophet standing in the holy place (let the reader understand), then those in Judea must flee to the mountains, a person on the housetop must not go down to get things out of his house, a person in the field must not return to get his cloak. Woe to pregnant women and nursing mother in those days. Pray that your flight not be in winter or on the sabbath, for at that time there will be the great tribulation, such as has not been since the beginning of the world until now, nor ever will be."

(Also Mark 13(14-23), Luke 21(20-24))

IMPORTANT NOTE: Jesus had foretold a big war in Israel (Judea) country at the time when prophet Daniel had predicted. While reading the book of the prophet Daniel I picked out two sentences (Daniel 8(13-14)) which Jesus had talked about; below is a comparison of the words of Jesus according to Matthew and the vision of prophet Daniel:

Matthew 24(15): "When you see *the desolating abomination* spoken of through Daniel the prophet standing in *the holy place* (let the reader understand)".

Daniel 8(13-14): I heard a holy one speaking, and another said to whichever one it was that spoke, "How long shall the events of this vision last concerning the daily sacrifice, *the desolating sin* which is placed there, *the sanctuary*, and the trampled host?" He answered him, "For two thousand three hundred evenings and mornings, then the sanctuary shall be purified."

The two books mention similar things. "The desolating abomination" in Matthew is equivalent to "the desolating sin" in Daniel. As well as "the holy place" in Matthew is equivalent to "the sanctuary" in Daniel:

The desolating abomination = The desolating sin
The holy place = The sanctuary

"Two thousand three hundred evenings and mornings", I believe this means year 2300; Jesus did tell us that, the year 2300 will be a starting point to the END TIME, and Israel (Judea) country will be lost again shortly after that. It does match "The 144,000 Seals" and "The Thousand-year Reign" mentioned in Revelation of St. John. "The Thousand-year Reign" for Christian Church is a period from year 1290 to year 2300. The year 1290 was the end of the last Crusade (Holy war), and "1290 days" in the vision of prophet Daniel 12(11).

_ Mark 13(7-8): "When you hear of wars and reports of wars do not be alarmed; such things must happen but it will not yet be the end. Nations will rise against nations and kingdom against kingdom. There will be earthquakes from place to place and there will be famines. These are beginning of the labor pains."

_ Luke 21(7-11): Then they asked him: "Teacher, when will this happen? And what sign will there be when all these things are about to happen?" He answered: "See that you not to be deceived for many will come in my name, saying, 'I am he, and the time has come.' Do not follow them! When you hear of wars and insurrection do not be terrified; for such things must happen first, but it will not immediately be the end." Then he said to them, "Nation will rise against nation, and kingdom against kingdom. There will be powerful earthquakes, famines, and plagues from place to place, and awesome sights and mighty signs will come from the sky."

* The happening of END DAY:
_ Matthew 24(29-31): "Immediately after tribulation of those days the sun will be darkened, and the moon will not give its light, and the stars will fall from the sky, and the power of the heavens will be shaken. And then the sign of the Son of man will appear in heaven, and the tribes of the earth will mourn, and they will see the Son of man coming upon the clouds of heaven with power and great glory. And he will send out his angels with a trumpet blast, and they will gather his elect from four winds, from one end of heaven to the other."

_ Luke 21(25-28): "There will be signs in the sun, the moon, and the stars, and on earth nations will be in dismay, perplexed by the roaring of the sea and the waves. People will die of fright in anticipation of what is coming upon the world, for power of the heavens will be shaken. And then they will see the Son of man coming in a cloud with power and great glory. But when these signs begin to happen, stand erect and raise your heads because your redemption is at hand."

Refer to Gospel of Matthew 24(3-44); Mark 13(1-37); Luke 17(22-37), 21(7-11), 21(25-33).

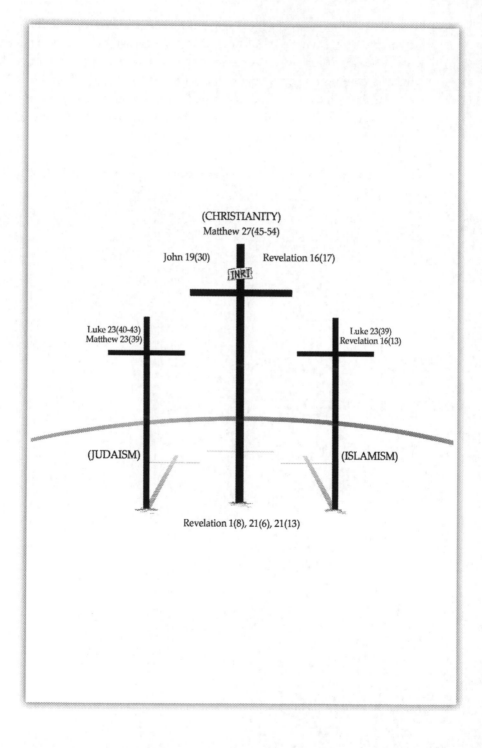

5.2   The END DAY with the Death of Jesus:

The image of the death of Jesus on Golgotha (place of the skull) was the image of the END DAY. Jesus was crucified in the middle of two criminals. According to Gospel of Luke 23(39-43): "Now one of the criminals hanging there reviled Jesus, saying, 'Are you not the Messiah? Save yourself and us.' The other, however, rebuked him, said in reply, 'Have you no fear of God; for you are subject to the same condemnation? And indeed, we have been condemned justly, for the sentence we received corresponds to our crimes, but his man has done nothing criminal.' Then he said, 'Jesus, remember me when you come into your kingdom.' He replied to him, 'Amen, I say to you, today you will be with me in paradise.'"

The question is why not one, three or four . . . criminals? We can explain that:

*   Jesus represented Christianity.
*   The criminal who reviled Jesus represented Islamism.
*   The criminal who asked Jesus to his kingdom represented Judaism. At END TIME, Judaism will return to Jesus as He said: "I tell you, you will not see me again until you say, 'Bless is he who comes in the name of the Lord.'" Matthew 23(39). Christianity, Islam and Judaism are the three main religions in the END DAY.
*   The Earthquakes, rain, lightning, and the veil of the sanctuary was torn in two from top to bottom, when Jesus died represented what will occur on the END DAY.
*   Jesus was crucified on Friday, so the END DAY will be on GOOD FRIDAY.

5.3   The END DAY according to the Book of the Prophet Daniel

The Prophet Daniel lived around 600 B.C. A young Jew was taken Babylon before the Jewish people were exiled to Babylon. Babylon was a stately capital of the Chaldeans Empire (modern day Iraq country). Daniel interpreted the dream of king Nebuchadnezzar, so the king advanced him to a high post and made him ruler of the whole province of Babylon. However, he always worshiped the God of Israel and never kneed down before the gods of Babylon. As a result, some of the Generals of Babylon urged the king to kill Daniel, but God helped him get out of danger. His book described some important events in Babylon, his vision about the exile of Jewish people, the fall of the Empire and the day the Jewish people returned to rebuild the Holy

Black Sea

Caspian Sea

Mediterranean Sea

Jewish captives bound for Babylon

Susa (Iran)

Jerusalem

Babylon (Iraq)

Babylonian Empire

Red Sea

City Jerusalem. He wrote very little about the END DAY, but his writings still contained very important information.

The Old Testament reflects onto the New Testament; the Jewish people reflects onto Christianity; Jerusalem reflects onto the kingdom of God after the END DAY. So, if one reads the Book of the Prophet Daniel contained in the Old Testament, one can find some hidden information concerning the END DAY.

   *   Daniel 8(13-17):

"I heard a holy one speaking and another said to whichever one that spoke: 'How long shall the events of this vision last concerning the daily sacrifice, the desolating sin which is placed there, the sanctuary, and the trampled host?' He answered him, 'for two thousand three hundred evenings and mornings, then the sanctuary shall be purified.'"

While I, Daniel, sought the meaning of the vision I had seen, a manlike figure stood before me, and on the Ulai I heard a human voice that cried out: "Gabriel, explain the vision to his man." When he came near where I was standing, I fell prostrate in terror, but he said to me, "understand, son of man, that vision refers to the end time."

   *   Daniel (12(1-13):

At that time there shall arise Michael, the great prince, guardian of your people; it shall be a time unsurpassed in distress since nations began until that time. At that time your people shall escape, everyone who is found written in the book. Many of those who sleep in the dust of the earth shall awake; some shall live forever, other shall be an everlasting horror and disgrace. But the wise shall shine brightly like the splendor of the firmament, and those lead the many to justice shall be the stars forever.

"As for you, Daniel, keep secret the message and seal the book until the end time: many shall fall away and evil shall increase."

I, Daniel, looked and saw two others, one standing on either bank of the river. One of them said to the man clothed in linen, who was upstream, "How long shall it be to the end of these appalling things?" The man clothed in linen, who was upstream lifted his right and left hands to heaven; and I heard him swear by him who lives forever that it should be for a year, two year, a half-year; and that, when the power of the destroyer of the holy people was brought to an end all these things should end. I heard, but I did not understand; so I asked, "My lord, what follow this?" "Go, Daniel,' he said', because the words are to be kept secret and sealed until the end time. Many shall be refined, purified, and tested, but the wicked shall prove wicked; none of them shall have understanding, but the wise shall have it. From the time that the daily sacrifice is abolished and the horrible abominations is set up, there shall be one thousand two hundred and ninety days. Blessed is the man who has patience and perseveres until the one thousand three hundred and thirty-five days. Go, take your rest, you shall rise for your reward at the end of days".

After read the above parts of book of prophet Daniel, now we have some numbers:
- 2300 evenings and mornings
- 1290 days
- 1335 days
- one year, two years, a half-year.
  We can explain the following:
  (1) From Jesus until Christian Church was settled in peace is the year 1290.
  (2) Peaceful and enjoyable time for Christianity from year 1290-2300.
  (3) Ready for END DAY in the year 2625 = (1290 + 1335).
  (4) Suffer time for Christianity is 3.5 years (1 + 2+.5). When the enemy attack Italy and Rome. Also suffer time for Jewish people in the war they lost their country.
  (5) The END DAY will be on GOOD FRIDAY year 2633:
  Year 2625 + 7 last years + 3.5 months
  In short, the book of prophet Daniel did not describe what warning signs, the process of happening before and during the END DAY, but he gave us very important numbers.

5.4 The END DAY in the Book of Revelation According to John

This book has been discussed quite a bit by scholars, prophets and scientists. Saint John lived in the first century. At the time Christians were pursued and persecuted by the Pharisees and the Roman Empire. He was exiled to the Rocky Island of Patmos, a Roman penal colony. His prophesy covers a long period of time from the first century to the END DAY. However, he wrote very little about exact dates when each event was to occur. It is very difficult to know when the END DAY will occur, but perhaps he described what will happen in order, so we might guess to the next one.

First, we will try to summarize and explain each chapter. Then we will combine them together to form an answer.

    *   Chapters 1, 2, 3 :

(a) Revelation 1(1-3): The revelation of Jesus Christ, which God gave to him, to show his servants what must happen soon. He made it known by sending his angel to his servant John, who give witness to the word of God and to the testimony of Jesus Christ by reporting what he saw. Blessed is the one who reads aloud and blessed are those who listen to this prophetic message and heed what is written in it, for the appointed time is near.

(b) Revelation 1(4-8): John, to the seven churches in Asia: grace to you and peace from him who is and who was and who is to come, and from the seven spirits before his throne, and from Jesus Christ, the faithful witness, the first born of the dead and ruler of the kings of the earth. To him who loves us and has freed us from our sins by his blood, who has made us into a kingdom, priest for his God and Father to him be glory and power forever (and ever), Amen.

> Behold, he is coming amid the cloud,
> and every eye will see him,
> even those who pierced him.
> All the people of the earth will lament him
> Yes. Amen.

"I am the Alpha and the Omega", say the Lord God, "the one who is and who was and who is to come, the almighty.

(c) Revelation 1(9-20): I, John, your brother, who share with you the distress, the kingdom, and the endurance we have in Jesus, found myself on the island called Patmos because I proclaimed God's words and gave testimony to Jesus. I was caught up in spirit on the Lord's day and heard behind me a voice as loud as a trumpet, which say, "Write on a scroll what you see and send it to the seven churches: to Ephesus, Smyrna, Pergamum, Thyatira, Sardis, Philadelphia, and Laodicea". Then I turned to see whoose voice it was that spoke to me, and when I turned, I saw seven gold lampstands and in the midst of the lampstands one like son of man, wearing an ankle-length robe, with a gold sash around his chest. The hair of his head was a white wool or

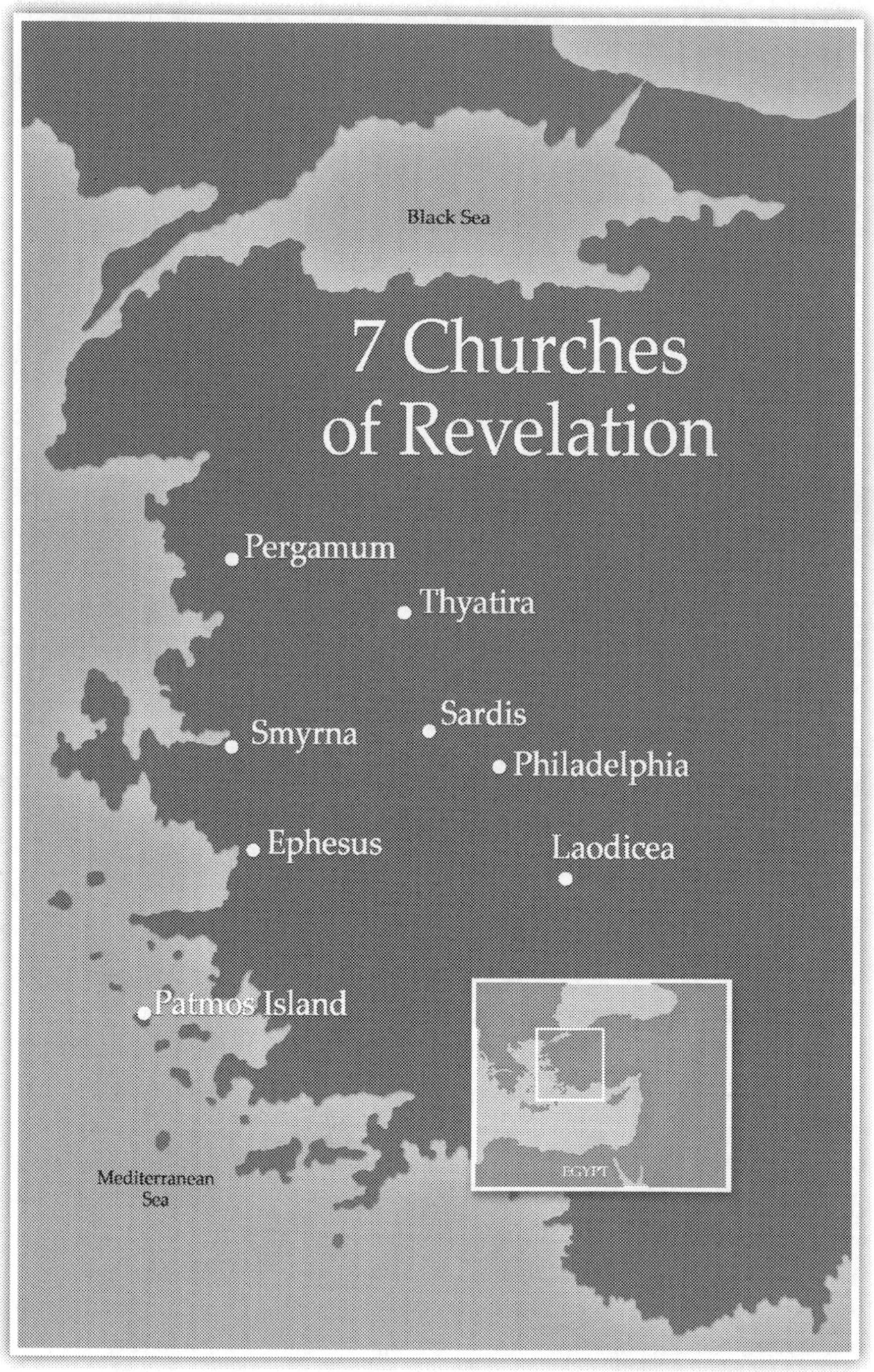
Black Sea
7 Churches
of Revelation
Pergamum
Thyatira
Sardis
Smyrna
Philadelphia
Ephesus
Laodicea
Patmos Island
EGYPT
Mediterranean
Sea

as snow, and his eyes were like a fiery flame. His feet were like polished brass refined in a furnace, and his voice was like the sound of rushing water. In his right hand he held seven stars. A sharp two-edge sword came out his mouth, and his face shone like the sun at its brightest.

When I caught sight of him, I fell down at his feet as though dead. He touched me with his right hand and said. "Do not be afraid, I am the first and the last, the one who lives, ones I was dead, but now I am alive forever and ever. I hold the key to death and the netherworld. Write down, therefore, what you have seen, and what is happening, and what will happen afterward. This is the secret meaning of the seven stars you saw in my right hand, and of the seven gold lampstands: the seven stars are the angels of the seven churches, and the seven lampstands are the seven churches.

* Chapter 2 and chapter 3 include seven letters to seven churches in Asia.

> **Explain:** *Chapter 1,2,3 describe the greeting, the first vision of John with Jesus, and Jesus commands John to send seven letters to seven churches in Asia. The mainly ideas of letters remind the churches patience and repentance. At that time, these seven churches locate in the West of Greek country. However, the first sign of END DAY will occur by suffering of the churches in some Asia countries in present day.*

* Chapter 4, 5 describe the vision of Heavenly worship, the very powerful God sit on the throne, holds the Seals in his right hand, and orders someone to open them; Jesus (a Lamb that seemed to have been slain) is only worthy one who has power to open the Seals.

* Chapter 6: The First Six Seals.
(1) The first seal: Then I watched while the Lamb broke open the first of seven seals, and I heard one of the four creatures cry out in a voice like thunder, "Come forward". I look, and there was a white horse, and its rider had a bow. He was given a crown, and he rode forth victorious to further his victories!
> **Explain:** *Beginning of END DAY, a new Empire is formed.*

(2) The second seal: When he broke open the second seal, I heard the second living creature cry out, "Come forward". Another the horse came out,

a red horse. Its rider was given power to take peace away from the earth, so that people would slaughter one another. And he was given a huge sword.

Explain: A big war occurs.

(3) The third seal: When he broke open the third seal, I heard the third living creature cry out, "Come forward". I looked, and there was a black horse, and its rider held a scale in his hand. I heard what seemed to be a voice in the midst of the four living creatures. It said, "A radiation of wheat cost a day's pay, and three rations of barley cost a day' pay. But do not damage the olive oil or the wine".

Explain: Starvation in the world but not at Western countries (do not damage the olive oil or the wine).

(4) The fourth seal: When he broke open the fourth seal, I heard the voice of the fourth living creature cry out, "Come forward". I looked and there was a pale horse. Its rider was named Death, and Hades accompanied him. They were given authority over a quarter of the earth to kill with sword, famine, and plague, and by means of the beast of the earth.

Explain: Death from many sources kill ¼ population of the earth.

(5) The fifth seal: When he broke open the fifth seal, I saw underneath the altar the souls of those who had been slaughtered because of the witness they bore to the word of God. They cried out in a loud voice, "How long will it be, holy and true master, before you sit in judgment and avenge our blood on the inhabitants of the earth?" Each of them was given a white robe, and they were told to be patient a little while longer until the number was filled of their fellow servants and brothers who were going to be killed as they had been.

Explain: At this time, many Christians are killed, persecuted by new Empire.

(6) The sixth seal: Then I watched while he broke open the sixth seal, and there was a great earthquake; the sun turned as black as dark sackcloth

and the whole moon became like blood. The stars in the sky fell to the earth like unripe figs shaken loose from the tree in a strong wind. Then the sky was divided like a torn scroll curling up, and every mountain and island was moved from its place. The kings of the earth, the nobles, the military offices, the rich, the powerful, and every slave and free person hid themselves in caves and among mountain crags. They cried out to the mountains and the rocks, Fall on us and hide us from the face of the one who sit on the throne and from the wrath of the Lamb, because the great day of their wrath has come and who can withstand it?"

Explain: A great earthquake never happen before.

* Chapter 7:
(1) The 144,000 Seals: After this I saw four angels standing at the four corner of the earth, holding back the four winds of the earth so that no wind could flow on land or sea or against any tree. Then I saw another angel come up from the East, holding the seal of the living God. He cried out in a loud voice to the four angels who were given power to damage the land and the sea, "Do not damage the land or the sea or the trees until we put the seal on the foreheads of the servants of our God."

I heard the number of those who had been marked with the seal, one hundred and forty-four thousand marked from every tribe of the Israelites: twelve thousand were marked from the tribe of Judah, twelve thousand from the tribe of Reuben, twelve thousand from the tribe of Gad, twelve thousand from the tribe of Asher, twelve thousand from the tribe of Naphtali, twelve thousand from the tribe of Manasseh, twelve thousand from the tribe of Simeon, twelve thousand from the tribe of Levi, twelve thousand from the tribe of Issachar, twelve thousand from the tribe of Zebulun, twelve thousand from the tribe of Joseph, and twelve thousand were marked from the tribe of Benjamin.

Explain: Jacob also named Israel had twelve sons, the twelve tribes : Reuben, Simeon, Levi, Judah, Dan, Naphtali, Gad, Asher, Issachar, Zebulun, Joseph, Benjamin. When the promise land was divided, the tribe of Levi had no part of land, they were special responsibility for worship God. Instead, the tribe of Joseph had two parts of land for his two sons Manasseh and Ephraim because he saved Jacob's family to Egypt from starvation.

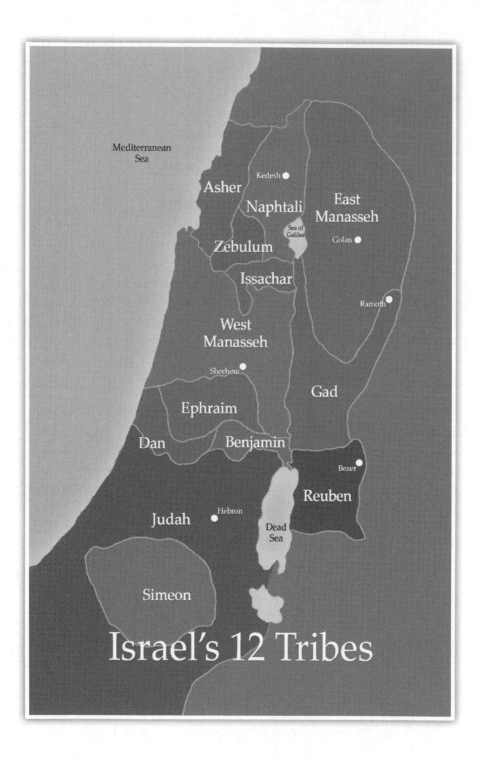

Israel's 12 Tribes

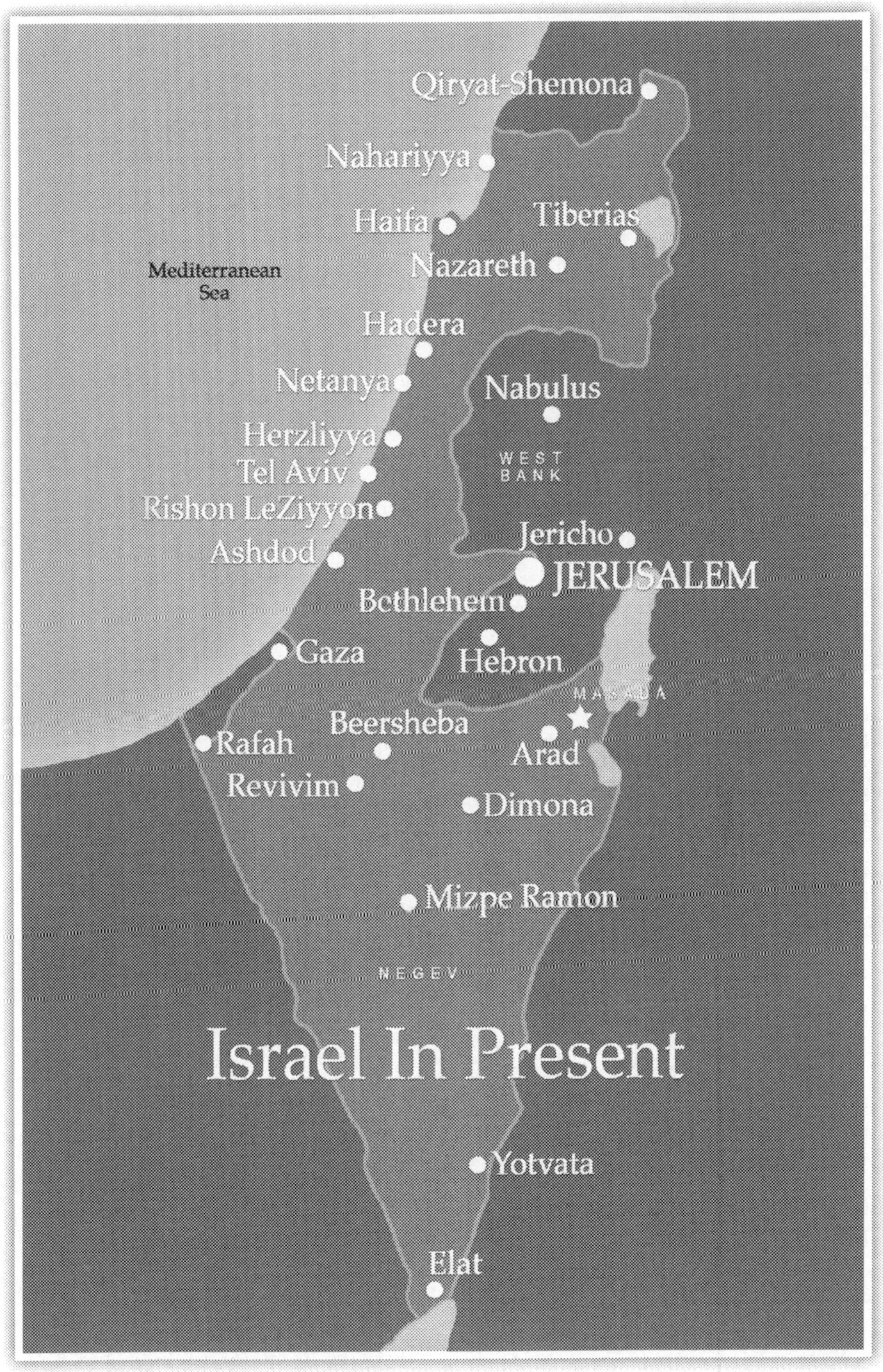
Qiryat-Shemona
Nahariyya
Haifa
Tiberias
Nazareth
Mediterranean Sea
Hadera
Netanya
Nabulus
Herzliyya
Tel Aviv
WEST BANK
Rishon LeZiyyon
Jericho
Ashdod
JERUSALEM
Bethlehem
Gaza
Hebron
Beersheba
Rafah
Arad
Revivim
Dimona
Mizpe Ramon
NEGEV
Israel In Present
Yotvata
Elat

In this chapter, the tribe of Dan was missing. The number one hundred and forty-four thousand in the Bible usually described the complete number, the symbolic of new Israel (note 7,4-9 of Revelation). Therefore, at this time, Israelites will lose their country again, except capital Tel Avis (the tribe of Dan) stills remain. The New Empires surround four sides of Israel country and then occupy it, except capital Tel Avis (Revelation 7(1): After this I saw four angels standing at the four corners of the earth, holding back the four winds of the earth so that no wind could flow on land or sea or against any trees).

(2) Triumph of the Elect: After this I had a vision of a multitude, which no one could count, from many nation, race, people, and tongue. They stood before the throne and before the Lamb, wearing white robes and holding palm branches in their hands. They cried out a loud voice:

> "Salvation comes from our God, who is
> seated on the throne
> and from the Lamb."

All the angels stood around the throne and around the elders and the four living creatures. They prostrated themselves before the throne, worship God and exclaimed:

> "Amen. Blessing and glory, wisdom and
> thanksgiving,
> honor, power, and might
> be to our God forever and ever. Amen."

Then one of the elders spoke up and said to me, "Who are these wearing white robes, and where did they come from?" I said to him, "My lord, you are the one to know." He said to me, "These are tho ones who have survived the time of great distress; they have washed their robes and made them white in the blood of the Lamb.

"For this reason they stand before God's
throne
and worship him day and night in his
temple
The one who sits on the throne will
shelter them.
They will not hungry or thirst anymore,
nor will the sun or any heat strike them.
For the Lamb who is in the center of the
throne will shepherd them
and lead them to springs of life-giving
water,
and God will wipe away every tear from
their eyes."

Explain: At this time, Christians are killed in many places.

*   Chapter 8:

(1) The Seven Trumpets: "When he broke open the seventh seal, there was silence in heaven for about half an hour. And I saw that the seven angels who stood before God were given seven trumpets.

Explain: After the Israelites lost their country, the world will peaceful for about half century.

(2) The Gold Censer: Another angel came and stood at the altar, holding a gold censer. He was given a great quantity of incense to offer, along with the prayers of all holy ones, on the gold altar that was before the throne. The smoke of the incense along with the prayers of holy ones went up before God from the hand of the angel. Then the angel took the censer, filled it with burning coals from the altar, and hurled it down to the earth. There were peals of thunder, rumblings, flashers of lightning, and an earthquake.

Explain: The war is broken again by conflict of religions.

(3) The First Four Trumpets: The seven angels who were holding the seven trumpets prepared to blow them.

_ When the first one blew his trumpet, there came hail and fire mixed with blood, which was hurled down to the earth. A third of the land was burned up, along with a third of trees and all green grass.

_ When the second angel blew his trumpet, something like a large burning mountain was hurled in to the sea. A third of the sea turned to blood, a third of the creatures living in the sea died, and a third of the ships were wrecked.

_When the third angel blew his trumpet, a large star burning like a torch fell from the sky. It fell on the third of the rivers and on the spring of water. The star was called "Wormwood," and a third of all water turned to wormwood. Many people died from this water, because it was made bitter.

_When the fourth angel blew his trumpet, a third of the sun, a third of the moon, and a third of the stars were struck, so that a third of them became dark. The day lost its light for a third of the time, as did the night.

Explain: *The first trumpet is a wave of missiles on land. The second trumpet is war on the seas. The third trumpet is chemical wars. The fourth trumpet is nuclear missiles.* * Chapter 9:

(1) The Fifth Trumpet: Then the fifth angel blew it trumpet, and I saw a star that had fallen from the sky to the earth. It was given the key for the passage to the abyss, and the smoke came up out of the passage like smoke from a huge furnace. The sun and the air were darkened by the smoke from the passage. Locusts came out of the smoke on the land, and they were given the same power as scorpions of the earth. They were told not to harm the grass of the earth or any plant or any tree, but only those who did not have the seal of God, on the forehead. They were not allowed to killed them but only to torment them for five months; the torment they inflicted was like that of a scorpion when it stings a person. During that time these people will seek death but will not find it, and they will long to die but death will escape them.

The appearance of the locusts was like that of horses ready for battle. On their heads they wore what looked liked crowns of gold; their faces were like human faces, and they had hair like human's hairs. Their teeth were like lions' teeth, and they had chests like iron breastplates. The sound of their wings was like the sound of many horse-drawn chariots racing into battle. They had tails like scorpions, with stingers; with their tails they had power to harm people for five months. They had as their king the angel of the abyss, whose name in Hebrew is Abaddon and Greek Apollyon. The first woe has passed, but there are to come.

> **Explain:** *Air Force drops bombs in Middle East for five months (not to harm the grass of the earth or any plant or any tree.)*

(2) The Sixth Trumpet: Then the sixth angel blew his trumpet, and I heard a voice coming from the (four) horns of the gold altar before God, telling the sixth angel who held the trumpet, "Release the four angels who are bound at the banks of the great river Euphrates". So the four angels were released, who were prepared for this hour, day, month, and year to kill a third of human race. The number of cavalry troops was two hundred million; I heard their number. Now in my vision this is how I saw the horses and their riders. They wore red, blue, and yellow breastplates, and the horses' heads were like heads of lions, and out of their mouths came fire, smoke, and sulfur. By these three plagues of fire, smoke, and sulfur that came out by their mouths a third of human race was killed. For the power of the horses is in their mouths and in their tails are like snakes, with heads that inflict harm.

The rest of human race, who were not killed by these plagues, did not repent of the work of their hands, to give up the worship of demons and idols made from gold, silver, bronze, stone, and wood, which cannot see or hear or walk. Nor did they repent of their murders, their magic potions, their unchastity, or their robberies.

> **Explain:** *A big battle at the river Euphrates with two million soldiers and their tanks kill one third of human race. The rest of human race who are not killed, they do not repent, keep doing bad things.*

*   Chapter 10: The Angel with the small scroll

Then I saw another mighty angel come down from heaven wrapped in a cloud, with a halo around his head; his face was like the sun and his feet were like pillar of fire. In his hand he held a small scroll that had been opened. He placed his right foot on the sea and his left foot on the land, and then he cried out in a loud voice as a lion roars. When he cried out, the seven thunders raised their voices, too. When the seven thunders had spoken, I was about to write it down; but I heard a voice from heaven say, "Seal up what the seven thunders have spoken, but do not write it down." Then the angel I saw on the sea and on the land raised his right hand to heaven and swore by the one who lives forever and ever, who created heaven and earth and sea and all that is in them, "There shall be no more delay. At the time when you hear the seventh angel blow his trumpet, the mysterious plan of God shall be fulfilled, as he promised to his servants the prophets."

Then the voice that I had heard from heaven spoke to me again and said, "Go, take the scroll that lies open in the hand of the angel who is standing on the sea and on the land. So I went up to the angel and told him to give me the small scroll. He said to me, "Take and swallow it. It will turn your stomach sour, but in your mouth it will taste as sweet as honey." I took small scroll from the angel's hand and swallow it. In my mouth it was like sweet honey, but when I had eaten it, my stomach turned sour. Then someone said to me, "You must prophesy again about many peoples, nations, tongues, and kings."

> **Explain:** *This is similar like prophet Ezekiel 3(3-4) at the time Jewish people were exiled to Babylon. In his vision, God gave Ezekiel a small scroll to eat and it as sweet as honey in his mouth. And God order him goes and speaks to all the house of Israel what God wanted them to do.*
>
> *The different vision of John was that his mouth was sweet but his stomach was sour. This means that, after the wars, people still not afraid God, they do not repent; even the Revelation of John has been told to the whole world, that why he felt sour in his stomach.*

* Chapter 11:

(a) The Two Witnesses: Then I was given a measuring rod like a staff and I was told, "Come and measure the temple of God and the altar, and count those who are worshiping in it. But exclude the outer court of the temple; do not measure it, for it has been handed over to the Gentiles, who will trample the holy city for forty two months. I will commission my two witnesses to prophesy for those twelve hundred and sixty days, wearing sackcloth."

These are the two olive trees and the two lampstands that stand before the Lord of the earth. If anyone wants to harm them, fire comes out of their mouths and devours their enemies. In this way, anyone wanting to harm them is sure to be slain. They have the power to close up the sky so that no rain can fall during the time of their prophesying. They also have power to turn water into blood and to afflict the earth with any plague as often as they wish.

When they have finished their testimony, the beast that comes up from the abyss will wage war against them and conquer them and kill them. Their corpses will lie in the main street of the great city, which has the symbolic names "Sodom" and "Egypt," where indeed their Lord was crucified. Those from every people, tribe, tongue, and nation will gaze on their corpses for three and half days, and they will not allow their corpses to be buried. The inhabitants of the earth will gloat over them and be glad and exchange gifts because these two prophets tormented the inhabitants of the earth.

But after the three and a half days, a breath of life from God entered them. When they stood on their feet, great fear fell from those who saw them. Then they heard a loud voice from heaven say to them, Come up here." So they went up to heaven in a cloud as their enemies look ed on. At the moment there was a great earthquake, and the tenth of the city fell in ruins. Seven thousand people were killed during the earthquake; the rest were terrified and gave glory to the God of heaven.

The second woe has passed, but the third is coming soon.

> **Explain:** *Enemy take over Italy for forty-two months and surround Rome for twelve hundred and sixty days (42 months= 1260days) then attack to Basilica of Saint Peter and Saint Paul. After three and half days, Rome will be restored.*

(b) The Seventh Trumpet: Then the seventh angel blew his trumpet. There were loud voices in heaven, saying, "The kingdom of the world now belong to our Lord and to his Anointed, and he will reign forever and ever." The twenty four elders who sat on their thrones before God prostrated themselves and worship God and said:

> "We give thanks to you, Lord God
> almighty,
> who are and who were.
> For you have assumed your great power
> and have established your reign.
> The nation raged, but your wrath has come,

> and the time for the dead to be judge,
> and to recompense your servant, the
> prophets,
> and the holy ones and those who fear your name,
> the small and the great alike,
> and destroy those who destroy the earth."

Then God's temple in heaven was opened, and the ark of his covenant could be seen in the temple. There were flashes of lighting, rumbling, and peals of thunder, an earthquake, and a violent hailstorm.

Explain: *Ready for the END DAY.*

* Chapter 12: The Woman and the Dragon:

A great sign appeared in the sky, a woman clothed with the sun, with the moon under her feet, and on her head a crown of twelve stars. She was with the child and wailed aloud in pain as she labored to give birth. Then another sign appear in the sky; it was a huge red dragon, with seven heads and ten horns, and on his heads were seven diadems. Its tail swept away a third of the stars in the sky and hurled them down to the earth. Then the dragon stood before the woman about to give birth, to devour her child when she gave birth. She gave birth to a son, a male child, destined to rule all the nations with an iron rod. Her child was caught up to God and his throne. The woman herself fled into the desert where she had a place prepared by God, that there she might be taken care of for twelve hundred and sixty days.

Then war broke out in heaven; Michael and his angels battled against the dragon. The dragon and its angels fought back, but they did not prevail and there was no longer any place for them in heaven. The huge dragon, the ancient serpent, who is called the Devil and Satan, who deceived the whole world, was thrown down to earth, and its angels were thrown down with it.

Then I heard a loud voice in heaven say:

> "Now have salvation and power come.
> and the kingdom of our God
> and the authority of his Anointed.
> For the accuser of our brothers is cast out,
> who accuses them before our God day and
> night.

They conquered him by the blood of the
Lamb
and by the word of their testimony;
love for life did not deter them from
death.
Therefore, rejoice, you heavens,
and you who dwell in them.
But woe to you, earth and sea,
for the Devil has come down to you in great fury,
for he knows he has but a short time."

When the dragon saw that it had been thrown down to the earth, it pursued the woman who had given birth to the male child. But the woman was given the two wings of the great eagle, so that she could fly to her place in the desert, where, far from the serpent, she was taken care of for a year, two years, and a half-year. The serpent, however, spewed a torrent of water out of his mouth after the woman to sweep her away with the current. But the earth helped the woman and opened its mouth and swallowed the flood that the dragon spewed out of its mouth. Then the dragon became angry with the woman and went off to wage war against the rest of her offspring, those who keep God's commandments and bear witness to Jesus. It took its position on the sand of the sea.

> **Explain:** *This chapter has few meanings:*
> _ *The powerful woman is virgin Mary, mother of Jesus, a*
> *new Eve. The huge red dragon is Satan or Devil. After*
> *Jesus, Satan Messengers was sent to earth for war; as*
> *God said to Satan serpent in the garden Eden:*
> > *"I will put enmity between you and the woman,*
> > *and between your offspring and her.*
> > *He will strike at your head,*
> > *while you strike at his heel."*
> > *Genesis 3(15)*
>
> _ *Red Dragon also means Communism. In the year 1917,*
> *virgin Mary appeared at Fatima of Portugal country*
> *(Fatima is same name one of daughter of Muhammad,*
> *the prophet of Islamism) with three children: Lucia dos*

Santos and her cousin Jacinta and Francisco Marto, on the 13th day of six consecutive months, starting on May 13th. Lucia described seeing a woman "brighter than the sun, shedding rays of light clear and stronger than a crystal ball filled with the most sparkling water and pierced by the burning rays of the sun." On October 13th, 1917 She made the miracle the sun dancing and falling down to earth in front of about seventy thousand people. Beside three prophesies: world war I, world war II, assassination of Pope John Paul II, she also gave to sister Lucia three secret messages on July 13, 1917: pray Rosary every day, Communion of Reparation on the first Saturdays (of months), and she said: "I shall come to ask for the Consecration of Russia to My Immaculate Heart. If people attend to my request, Russia will be converted and the world will have peace. And in the end, my Immaculate Heart will triumph. The holly Father will consecrate Russia to Me, and she will be converted, and a period of peace will be granted to the world."

This was right to Revelation of Saint John: "The earth helped the woman and opened its mouth and swallowed the flood . . ." by people pray Rosary every day.

_*This chapter also complements for chapter 11, the woman is image of Head of Catholic church in Rome. Enemy will take over Italy and surround Rome at Christmas time (she was with child and wailed aloud in pain as she labored to give birth), the Pope has to fly to a safe place for three and a half-year.*

(3.5 years = 42 months = 1260 days)

*   Chapter 13:

(1) The First Beast: Then I saw a beast come out of the sea with ten horns and seven heads; on its horns were ten diadems, and on his heads blasphemous name(s). The beast I saw was like a leopard, but it had feet like a bear's, and its mouth was like the mouth of a lion. To it the dragon gave its own power and throne, along with great authority. I saw that one

of its head seemed to have been mortally wounded, but this mortal wound was healed. Fascinated, the whole world followed after the beast. They worshiped the dragon because it gave its authority to the beast; they also worshiped the beast and said: "Who can compare with the beast or who can fight against it?"

The beast was given a mouth uttering proud boasts and blasphemies, and it was given authority to act for forty-two months. It opened its mouth to utter blasphemies against God, blaspheming his name and his dwelling and those who dwell in heaven. It was also allowed to wage war against the holy ones and conquer them, and it was granted authority over every tribe, people, tongue, and nation. All the inhabitants of the earth will worship it, all whose names were not written from the book of life, which belongs to the Lamb who was slain.

> Whoever has ears ought to hear these
> words
> Anyone destined for captivity goes into
> captivity.
> Anyone destined to be slain by the sword
> shall be slain by the sword.
> Such is the faithful endurance of the holy ones.

Explain: *The leader of enemy who attack Italy and Rome for forty-two months as in chapter 11. All people in the world follow him except Christianity.*

(2) The Second Beast: Then I saw another beast come up out of the earth, it had two horns like a lamb's but spoke like a dragon. It wielded all authority of the first beast in its sight and made the earth an its inhabitants worship the first beast, whose mortal wound had been healed. It performed great signs, even making fire come down from heaven to earth in the sight of everyone. It deceived the inhabitants of the earth with the signs it was allowed to perform in the sight of the first beast, telling them to make an image for the beast who had been wound by the sword and revived. It was then permitted to breathe life into the beast's image, so that the beast's image could speak and [could] have anyone who did not worship it put to death. It forced all the people, small and great, rich and poor, free and slave, to be given a stamped image on their right hand or their foreheads, so that no one

could buy or sell except one who had the stamped image of the beast's name or the number that stood for its name.

Wisdom is needed here; one who understands can calculate the number of the beast, for it is a number that stands for a person. His number is six hundred and sixty-six.

> *Explain: The second beast worships the first beast describing the power of a extreme group which relates to a religion. At this time, with high technology, they can stamp a tiny device into human body to control people. The second Beast will cause the END DAY.*

* Chapter 14:

(1) The Lamb's Companions: Then I looked and there was the Lamb standing on Mount Zion, and with him a hundred and forty-four thousand who had his name and his Father's name written on their foreheads. I heard a sound from heaven like the sound of rushing water or a loud peal of thunder. The sound I heard was like that harpist playing their harps. They were singing [what seemed to be] a new hymn before the throne, before four living creatures and the elders. No one could learn this hymn except the hundred and forty-four thousand who had been ransomed from the earth. These are they who were not defiled with women; they are virgins and these are the ones who follow the Lamb wherever he goes. They have been ransomed as the first fruits of the human race for God and the Lamb. On their lips no deceit has been found; they are unblemished.

> *Explain: The number one hundred forty-four thousand usually describe a huge and complete number in the Bible. So, at this time, the Catholic church will allow the married priests.*

(2) The Three Angels: Then I saw another angel flying high over head, with everlasting good news to announce to those who dwell on earth, to every nation, tribe, tongue, and people. He said in a loud voice, "Fear God and give him glory, for his time has come to sit in judgment. Worship him who make heaven and earth and sea and spring water."

A second angel followed, saying:
"Fallen, fallen is Babylon the great,
that made all the nation drink
the wine of her licentious passion."

A third angel followed them and said in a loud voice, "Anyone who worship the beast or its image, or accepts its mark on forehead or hand, will also drink the wine of God's fury, poured full strength into the cup of his wrath, and will be tormented in burning sulfur before the holy angels and before the Lamb. The smoke of the fire that torments them will rise forever and ever, and there will be no relief day or night for those who worship the beast or its image or accept the mark of its name." Here is what sustains the holly ones who keep God's commandment and their faith in Jesus.

I heard a voice from heaven say, "Write this: Blessed are the dead who die in the Lord from now on." "Yes," said the Spirit, "let them find rest from their labors, for their works accompany them."

Explain: *Three leaders of the world call for the united many countries to fight with the Beast Empire.*

(3) The harvest of the Earth: Then I looked and there was a white cloud, and sitting on the cloud one who looked like son of man, with a gold crown in his head and a sharp sickle in his hand. Another angel came out of the temple, crying out in a loud voice to the one sitting on the cloud, "Use your sickle and reap the harvest, for the time to reap has come, because the earth's harvest is fully ripe." So the one who was sitting on the cloud swung his sickle over the earth, and the earth was harvested.

Then another angel came out of the temple in heaven who also had a sharp sickle. The another angel [came] from the altar, [who] was in charge of the fire, and cried out in a loud voice to the one who had the sharp sickle, "Use your sharp sickle and cut the cluster from the earth's vines, for its grapes are ripe." so the angel swung his sickle over the earth and cut the earth's vintage. He threw it into the great wine press of God' fury. The wine press was trodden outside the city and blood poured out of the wine press to the height of a horse's bridle for two hundred miles.

Explain: *Describe the END TIME, Jesus harvest the earth, every body include Christians (earth's vine). Jesus said: "I am the vine, you are the branches, whoever remain in me and I in him will bear much fruit, because without me you can do nothing." John 15(5).*

*   Chapter 15: The Seven Last Plagues

Then I saw in heaven another sign, great and awe-inspiring: seven angels with the seven last plagues, for through them God's fury is accomplished.

Then I saw something like a sea of glass mingled with fire. On the sea of glass were standing those who had won the victory over the beast and its image and the number that signified its name. They were holding God's harps, and they sang the song of Moses, the servant of God, and the song of the Lamb:

> "Great and wonderful are your works,
> Lord God almighty.
> Just and true are your ways,
> O king of the nations.
> Who will not fear you, Lord,
> or glorify your name?
> For you alone are holy.
> All the nations will come
> and worship before you,
> for your righteous acts have been
> revealed."

After this I had another vision. The temple that is the heavenly tent of testimony opened, and the seven angels with the seven plagues came out of the temple. They were dressed in clean white linen, with a gold sash around their chests. One of the four living creatures gave the seven angels gold bowls filled with the fury of God, who lives forever and ever. Then the temple became so filled with smoke from God's glory and might that no one could enter it until the seven plagues of the seven angels had been accomplished.

Explain: *The Beast's army attack, kill many soldiers of the United countries' army, then the war is broken.*

*   Chapter 16: The Seven Bowls

I heard a loud voice speaking from the temple to the seven angels, "Go and pour out the seven bowls of God's fury upon the earth."

_ The first angel went and poured out his bowl on the earth. Festering and ugly sores broke out on those who had mark of the beast or worshiped its image.

_ The second angel poured out his bowl on the sea. The sea turned to blood like that from the corpse; every creatures living in the sea died.

_ The third angel poured his bowl on the rivers and the spring water. These also turned to blood. Then I heard the angel in charge of ware say:

> "You are just, O Holy One,
> who are and who were,
> in passing this sentence.
> For they have shed the blood of the holly
> ones and the prophets,
> and you [have] given them blood to drink;
> it is what they deserve."
> Then I heard the altar cry out,
> "Yes, Lord God almighty,
> your judgment s are true and just."

_ The fourth angel poured his bowl on the sun. It was given the power to burn people with fire. People were burned by the scorching heat and blasphemed the name of God who had power over these plagues, but they did not repent or give him glory.

_ The fifth angel poured out his bowl on the throne of the beast. Its kingdom was plunged into darkness, and people bit their tongues in pain and blasphemed the God of heaven because their pains and sores. But they did not repent of their works.

_The sixth angel emptied his bowl on the great river Euphrates. Its water was dried up to prepare the way for the kings of the East. I saw three unclean spirits like frogs come from the mouth of the dragon, from the mouth of the beast, and from the mouth of the false prophets. These were demonic spirits who performed signs. They went out to the kings of the whole world to assemble them for the battle on the great day of God the almighty. ("Behold, I am coming like a thief." Blessed is the one who watches and keeps his clothes ready, so that he not go naked and people see him exposed.) They then assembled the kings in the place that is named Armageddon in Hebrew.

_ The seventh angel poured his bowl into the air. A loud voice came out of the temple from the throne, saying, "It is done." Then there were lightning flashes, rumblings, and peals of thunder, and a great earthquake. It was such a violent earthquake that there has never been one like it since the human race began on earth. The great city split into three parts, and the gentile cities fell. But God remembered great Babylon, giving it the cup filled with the wine of his fury and wrath. Every island fled, and mountains disappeared. Large hailstones like huge weights came down from the sky on people, and they blasphemed God for the plague of hail because this plague was so severe.

Explain: The first bowl, second bowl, third bowl and fourth bowl are the attack of the United countries to the Beast's countries; and then people are suffer by the Beast's governments (fifth bowl). After that, the Beast and their religion leaders assemble the big army to the battle of Armageddon (Middle East). At last God use a great earthquake and asteroids to destroy the whole world. END DAY.

* Chapter 17, 18, 19:

Explain:
_ *Describe the great Babylon city about the year 600B.C. (modern Iraq country): rich, power and sins. The fall of Empires and the return of Jewish to rebuild Jerusalem.*
_*Describe the power, rich of Roman Empires who kill many Christians. The fall of Roman Empires and the victory and growing of Christianity.*
_ *Describe our material world like the Babylon city, will be destroyed in the END DAY, and the happiness for people who are selected by Jesus.*
_ *The King of Kings: Describe the Holly War in the 11th,12th,13th century.*

* Chapter 20:
(1) The Thousand-year Reign: Then I saw an angel come down from heaven, holding in his hand the key to the abyss and a heavy chain. He seized

the dragon, the ancient serpent, which is the Devil or Satan, and tied it up for a thousand years and threw it into the abyss, which he locked over it and sealed, so that it could no longer lead the nations astray until the thousand years are completed. After this, it is to be released for a short time.

Then I saw thrones; those who sat on them were entrusted with judgment. I also saw the souls of those who had been beheaded for their witness to Jesus and for the word of God, and who had not worshiped the beast or its image, or had accepted its mark on their foreheads or hands. They came to life and they reigned with Christ for a thousand years. The rest of the dead did not come to life until the thousand years were over. This is the first resurrection. Blessed and holy is the one who shares in in the first resurrection, The second death has no power over these; they will be priests of God and of Christ, and they will with him for [the] thousand years.

When the thousand years are completed, Satan will be released from his prison. He will go out to deceive the nations at the four corners of the earth, Gog and Magog, to gather them for battle; their number is like the sand of sea. They invaded the breadth of the earth and surrounded the camp of the holy ones and the beloved city. But fire came down from heaven and consumed them. The Devil who had led them astray was thrown into the pool of fire and sulfur, where the beast and the false prophet were. There they will be tormented day and night forever and ever.

> **Explain:** *Christians were persecuted by Pharisees and Roman Empires from the beginning of the church and then Holy War with Islamism until around year 1290. From year 1290, Christians have a thousand years peaceful to growth until the year 2300. During this time, the church has been beatified and canonized for many Saints and say Mass to honest them; the souls who died and witness for Jesus.*(They came to life and they reigned with Christ for a thousand years). *After year 2300, Satan will be released then the world will be trouble, and the church will be suffer to END DAY.*

(2) The Large White Throne: Next, I saw a large white throne and the one who was sitting on it. The earth and the sky fled from his presence and there was no place for them. I saw the dead, the great and the lowly, standing before the throne, and scroll was opened, the book of life. The dead were judged according to their deeds, by what was written in the scrolls. The sea

gave up its dead; then Death and Hades were thrown into the pool of fire. (This pool of fire is the second death.) Anyone whose name was not found written in the book of life was thrown into the pool of fire.

> **Explain:** *Jesus sits on the large white throne to judge everyone on the END DAY.*

* Chapter 21, 22:
The New Heaven and the New Earth.
The New Jerusalem.

> **Explain:** *These two chapter describe the good people will live happy with God in Heaven forever and ever, the bad people will be thrown to the pool of fire and sulfur, which is the second death.*

* EPILOGUE :
And he said to me, "These words are trustworthy and true, and the Lord, the God of prophetic spirits, sent his angel to show his servants what must happened soon." "Behold, I am coming soon." Blessed is the one who keeps the prophetic message of this book.

It is I, John, who heard and saw these things, and when I heard and saw them I fell down to worship at the feet of the angel who showed them to me. But he said to me, "Don't! I am a follow servant of yours and of your brothers the prophets and of those who keep the message of this book. Worship God."

Then he said to me, "Do not seal up the prophetic words of this book, for the appointed time is near. Let the wicked still act wickedly, and the filthy still be filthy. The righteous must still do right, and the holy still be holy."

"Behold, I am coming soon. I bring with me the recompense I will give to each according to his deeds. I am the Alpha and the Omega, the first and the last, the beginning and the end."

Blessed are they who wash their robes so as to have the right for the tree of life and enter the city through its gates. Outside are the dogs, the sorcerers, the unchaste, the murders, the idol-worshipers, and all you love and practice deceit.

"I, Jesus, send my angel to give you this testimony for the churches. I am the root and offspring of David, the bright morning star."

The Spirit and the bride say, "Come." Let the hearer say, "Come." Let the one who thirsts come forward, and the one who wants it receive the gift of life-giving water.

I warn everyone who hears the prophetic words in this book: If anyone adds to them, God will add to him the plagues described in this book, and if anyone takes away from the words in this prophetic book, God will take away his share in the tree of life and in the holy city described in this book.

The one who gives this testimony say, "Yes, I am coming soon." Amen! Come, Lord Jesus!

The grace of the lord Jesus be with all.

> **Explain:** *Saint John wanted everyone seriously about the truth of prophetic words in the Revelation Book.*

5.5 THE END DAY IN THE BOOK OF PROPHET EZEKIEL

Prophet Ezekiel was one of exiles deported by Nebuchadnezzar in 597B.C. To Babylon. He was the first prophet to receive the call to prophesy outside the Holy Land. Most of his prophesy about what will be happened for Jewish people, their country Israel, some countries in the same region, and the day of his people return to rebuild Jerusalem.

In chapter 38 and 39, he prophesied against *Gog and Magog* what we see in the book Revelation to Saint John 20(8). *Gog and Magog* were people who lived North of Israel and surround Black sea, they will against Israel in the END DAY.

The following are chapters 38 and 39 in the book of prophet Ezekiel:

* Chapter 38:

(1) First Prophesy against *Gog*: Thus the word of the Lord came to me. Son of man, turn toward *Gog (the land of Magog)*, the chief prince of Meshech and Tubal, and prophesy against him. Thus says the Lord God: See! I am coming at you, *Gog*, chief prince of Meshech and Tubal. I will lead you forth with all your army, horses and riders all handsomely outfitted, a great horde with bucklers and shields, all of them carrying swords: Persia, Cush, and Put with them (all with shields and helmets), Gomer with all its troops, Beth-to-garmah from the recesses of the north with all its troops, many people with you. Prepare yourself, be ready, you and all your horde assembled about

you, and be at my disposal. After many days you will be mustered (in the last years, you will come) against a nation which has survived the swords, which has been assembled from many people (on the mountains of Israel which were long a ruin), which has been brought forth from among the peoples and all whom now dwell in security. You shall come up like a sudden storm, advancing like a cloud to cover the earth, you and all your troops and the many people with you.

Thus say the Lord God: At that time thoughts shall arise in your mind, and you shall devise and evil scheme: "I will go up against a land of open villages and attack the peaceful people who are living in security, all of them living without walls, having neither bars nor gates, to plunder and pillage, turning my hand against the ruins that were repeopled and against a people gathered from the nations, a people concerned with cattle and goods, who dwell at the navel of the earth." Sheba and Dedan, the merchants of Tarshish and all her young lions shall ask you: "Is it for plunder that you have come? Is it for pillage that you have summoned your horde, to carry off silver and gold, to take away cattle and goods, to seize much plunder?"

Thus say the Lord god: It is of you that I spoke in ancient times through my servants, the prophet of Israel, who prophesied in those days that I would bring you against them. But on that thay, the day when Gog invades the land of Israel, say the Lord God, my fury shall be aroused. In my anger and in my jealousy, in my fiery wrath, I swear: On that day there shall be a great shaking upon the land of Israel. Before me shall tremble the fish of the sea and the bird of the air, the beasts of the field and all the reptiles that crawl upo9n the ground, and all men who are on the land. Mountains shall be overturned, and cliffs shall tumble, and every wall shall fall to the ground. Against him I will summon every terror, say the Lord God, every man's sword against his brother. I will hold judgment with him in pestilence and bloodshed, flooding rain and hailstones, fire and brimstone, I will rain upon him, upon his troops, and upon many peoples with him. I will prove my greatness and holiness and make myself known in the sight of many nations; thus they shall know that I am the Lord.

(2) Second Prophesy against *Gog*: Therefore prophesy, son of man, and say to *Gog*: Thus say the Lord God: When my people Israel are dwelling in security, will you not bestir yourself and come from your home in the recesses of the north, you and many peoples with you, all mounted on horses, a great horde and mighty army? You shall come up against my people Israel like a cloud covering the land. *In the last days I will bring you against my land, that*

the nations may know of me, when in their sight I prove my holiness through you. O Gog.

*   Chapter 39: Third Prophesy against *Gog*:

Now son of man, prophesy against Gog in these words: Thus say the Lord God: See! I am coming at you, *Gog*, chief prince of Meshech and Tubal. I will turn you about, I will urge you on, and I will make you come up from the recesses of the north; I will lead you against the mountains of Israel. Then I will strike the bow from your left hand, and make the arrows drop from your right. Upon the mountains of Israel you shall fall, you and all your troops and the people who are with you. To the birds of prey of every kind and to the wild beast I am giving you to be eaten. On the open field you shall fall, for I have decreed it, say the Lord God:

I will send fire upon Magog and upon those who live security in the coast land; thus they shall know that I am the Lord. I will make my holy name known among my people Israel; I will no longer allow my holy name to be profaned. Thus the nations shall know that I am the Lord, the Holy One in Israel. Yes, It is coming and shall be fulfilled, say the Lord God. This is the day I have decreed.

The shall those who live in the cities of Israel go out and burn weapons: (shield and bucklers), bows and arrows, clubs and lances; for seven years they shall make fires with them. They shall not have to bring in wood from the fields or cut it down in the forests, for they shall make fires with the weapons. Thus they shall plunder those who plundered them, say the Lord God.

On that day I will give *Gog* for his tomb a well-known place in Israel, the Valley of Abarim east of the sea (it is blocked to travelers). *Gog* shall be buried there with all his horde, and it shall be named "Valley of Hamon-gog." To purify the land, the house of Israel shall need seven months to bury them. All the people of the land shall bury them and gain renown for it, when I reveal my glory, say the Lord God. Men shall be permanently employed to pass through the land burying those who lie unburied, so as to purify the land. For seven months they shall keep searching. When the pass through, should they see a human bone, let them put up a marker beside it, until others have buried it in the Valley of Hamon-gog. (also the name of the city shall be Hamonah). Thus the land shall be purified.

As for you, son of man, say the Lord God, say to birds of every kind and to all the wild beasts: Come together, from all sides gather for the slaughter on the mountains of Israel: you shall have flesh to eat and blood to drink.

You shall eat the flesh of warriors and drink the blood of princes of the land (rams, lambs, and goats, bullocks, fatlings of Bashan, all of them). From the slaughter which I will provide for you, you shall eat fat until you are filled and drink blood until you are drunk. You shall be filled at my table with horses and riders, with warriors and soldiers of every kind, say the Lord God.

Explain: Chapter 38, 39 in the book of prophet Ezekiel foretold the victory of Israel people in the battle when Gog and Magog attack their land in the old time. And it also provides the information explaining the people who represent Gog and Magog in the Revelation of Saint John.

5.6   THE COMBINATION

In this part, we will discuss two points: Who are leaders of people cause the END DAY and the progress to END DAY.

a)   Who Cause The END DAY?

(1) Revelation 16(13-14): "I saw three unclean spirits like frog come from the mouth of dragon, from the mouth of the beast, and from the mouth of the false prophet. These were demonic spirit who performed signs. They went out to the king of the world to assemble them for the battle on the great day of God the mighty".

Explain: Leaders who are evil, powerful and from a religion.

(2) Revelation 20(8): "He will go out to deceive the nations at four corners of the earth, Gog and Magog, together them for battle; their number is like the sand of the sea."

(3) Ezekiel 38(1-6): Described Gog and Magog were counties from north of Israel and surround the Black sea.

Explain: Gog and Magog are Arab countries now.

(4) Ezekiel 38(16): "You shall come up against my people Israel like a cloud covering the land. In the last day I will bring you against my land, that the nations may know of me, when in their sight I prove my holiness through you, O Gog."

(5) The image the death of Jesus on the cross between two criminals showed that, it will have big conflict between three remain mainly religions Christianity, Islamism and Judaism in the END DAY.

(6) Matthew 13(24-30): "Jesus proposed another parable to them, "The kingdom of heaven may be likened to a man who sowed good seed in his field. While everyone was asleep, his enemy came and sowed weeds all through the wheat, and then went off. When the crop grew and bore fruit, the weeds appeared as well. The slavers of the householder came to him and said, "Master, did you not sow good seed in your field? Where have the weed come from?" He answer, "An enemy has done this." His slaves said to him, "Do you want us to go and pull them up?" He replied, "No, if you pull up the weeds you might up root the wheat along with them. Let them grow together until harvest; then harvest time I will say to the harvesters, "First collect the weeds and tie them in bundles for burning; but gather the wheat into my barn."

> **Explain:** *The man who sowed the good seed is Jesus, the enemy who sowed the weeds came after Jesus.*

(7) Matthew 13(36-43): Then, dismissing the crowds, he went into the house. His disciples approach him and said, "Explain to us the parable of the weeds in the field." He said in reply, "He who sows good seed is the Son of Man, the field is the world, the good seed are the children of the kingdom. The weeds are the children of the evil one, and the enemy who sow them is the devil. The harvest is the end of the age, and the harvesters are angels. Just as weeds are collected and burned (up) with fire, so will it be at the end of the ages. The son of Man will send his angels, and they will collect out of his kingdom all who cause others to sin and all evildoers. They will throw them into the fiery furnace, where there will be walling and grinding of teeth. Then the righteous will shine like the sun in the kingdom of their Father. Whoever has ears ought to hear.

(8) Matthew 7(15-20): Jesus said: "Beware of false prophets, who come to you in sheep's clothing, but underneath are ravenous wolves. By their fruits you will know them. Do people pick grapes from thorn bushes, or figs from thistles? Just so, every good tree bears good fruit, and a rotten tree bears bad fruit. A good tree can not bear bad fruit nor can a rotten tree bear good fruit. Every tree that does not bear good fruit will be cut down and thrown into the fire. So by their fruits you will know them."

(9) "The Truth about Muhammad" of author Robert Spencer page 179-180: "Jesus will set things right at the end of the world. According to Islamic eschatology, He will return to end the dhimmi status of non-Muslims in Islamic societies_ not by initiating a new era of quality and harmony, but by abolishing Christianity and imposing Islam upon everyone. As Muhammad explained:

'By Him in Whose Hand my soul is, surely (Jesus)
the son of Mary will soon descent amongst you
and will judge mankind justly (as a just Ruler);
he will break the Cross and kill the pigs and
there will be no Jizya (i.e. taxation taken from non-Muslims)'

Another tradition put it this way: 'He will break the Cross, kill swine, and abolish Jizya. Allah will perish all religions except Islam.' And another hadith has Muhammad saying: 'How will you be when the son of Mary(i.e. Jesus) descends amongst you and he will judge people by the Law of the Qur'an and not by the law of Gospel'.

The Jews, meanwhile, will in the end times fare little better. Muhammad said: 'The last hour would not come unless the Muslims will fight against the Jews and the Muslims would kill them until the Jews would hide themselves behind a stone or a tree and a stone or a tree would say: 'Muslim, or the servant of Allah, there is a Jew behind me; come and kill him.'"

> *Explain: All (1), (2), (3), (4), (5), (6), (7), (8), (9) above indicate that, one extreme group of Islamism will cause the END DAY.*

b)   The Progress to END DAY:

After we read the book of prophet Daniel, the words of Jesus, the image Death of Jesus on the Golgotha Hill, the Revelation of Saint John, and the book of prophet Ezekiel, we are getting an answer for the END DAY. As we know that, the book of prophet Daniel gave us the times and the Revelation of Saint John gave us the progress to the END DAY, from the time of Jesus:

*   Christianity was persecuted by Pharisees and Roman Empires from the Death of Jesus, and also from the year 610 by Islamism until the Holy War over in the year 1290.

* A Thousand-year reign from 1290-2300, peaceful and joyful for Christianity expand to the whole world. After the year 2300, Satan will be released and disaster will begin to the END DAY.
* After year the year 2300, a new Empires from Islamism occupy Asia countries and the Christian churches in Asia will be suffer (first seal, white horse).
* War is broken in Asia countries (second seal, red horse).
* Starvation in the world (third seal, black horse), but not in Western countries (but do not damage the olive oil or the wine).
* Death by many sources killed ¼ population of the world (fourth seal, green horse).
* Christianity are slaughtered in Asia countries (fifth seal).
* Israel country will be lost again, except the capital Tel-Avis stills remain (missing tribe Dan in The 144,000 Seals).
* Christians are killed in many places (Triumph of the Elect).
* Peace for about half century and then the war is broken (silent in heaven for about half an hour).
* The Empire and Western countries attack each other by missiles on land, on the sea, chemical weapons and even nuclear missiles (4 trumpets).
* Air war in Middle East (fifth trumpet).
* Battle at the river Euphrates with two hundred million troops kills 1/3 human race (six trumpet).
* Peace for a while, but people of the world do not repent, they keep do sins and reject the warning of the church.
* The Empire takes over Italy at Christmas time and surround Rome for forty-two months (42 months = 1260 days = 3.5 years). The Pope has to fly to a safe place for 3.5 years. Then they attack Rome. After three and half days, Rome will be restored and enemy (first Beast) withdraws.
* Catholic church allows the priest has wife.
* Leaders of Western countries (The Three Angels) meeting to fight with the Beast.
* The last war in the year 2625, "The Harvest of the Earth" (2625 = 1290 + 1335). "The Seven Last Plagues" for the last seven years, the second Beast's army attack and kill many soldiers of Western's army, then the war is broken.

* The Western's countries attack to the Empire's countries very heavy (four bowls).
* Muslims are suffer by the Empire (the Beast's governments), (fifth bowl).
* The Empire's leaders assemble their army for the last battle of Armageddon (sixth bowl).
* God use earthquakes, asteroids to destroy the whole world (seventh bowl).
* The END DAY: Good Friday of the year 2633.

$$(2625 + 7 + 3.5 \text{ months})$$

God said: "I am the Alpha and the Omega, the first and the end."
{ Revelation 1(8), Revelation 21(6), Revelation 22(13) }.

Maybe God also give us a symbolic meaning for the special number 2633:

Capital:	A	Ω
Low case	α	ω

For hand writing:
_ Low case of "alpha" looks like the number "2", and its reverse side looks like the number "6".
_ Low case of "omega" looks like the number "3" at position 90 degrees.

Therefore: alpha alpha omega omega
              2   6   3   3

The story of Creation in the Bible from the year 4,000 B.C., then the END YEAR is 6633 from the beginning, also right with "alpha" and "omega".

Also:
* The year "33" Jesus was crucified.
* The year "632" Muhammad died at "62" years old.
* From the year "632" to the year "2632" is a period of 2000 years.

CHAPTER 6

THE CONCLUSION

There is one God, and God created everything. He made humankind very complex. We have free will to think, to say and to act. We are all children of Adam and Eve, but because we are "bouncing" within our Natural Universe and between God's Spirit and Evil Spirit, we create conflicts within individual, family, village, country, religion and world. As we get closer to the END DAY, the "bouncing" becomes faster, stronger and more violent, eventually destroying ourselves. Then God will end the world on Good Friday Year 2633. This date was hidden in the book of the prophet Ezekiel, the book of the prophet Daniel, the Revelation of Saint John, the Words of Jesus and the Death of the Lord Jesus Christ on Golgotha Hill. According to the Bible, He will be back to judge the whole world at END TIME.

* The END DAY must come as Jesus said: *"Heaven and Earth will pass away, but my words will not pass away."* Matthew 24(35).

* The END DAY is end of the war between Jesus and Satan as God said in the Garden Eden with the Satan serpent:

> "I will put enmity between you and the
> woman,
> and between your offspring and hers;
> He will strike at your head,
> while you strike at his heal."
> Genesis 3(15)

* The END DAY is the day that God feels too enough time for the Words of Jesus are taught everywhere in the world.
Matthew 24(14): *"And this gospel of the kingdom will be preached throughout the world as a witness to all nations, and then the end will come."*

* The END DAY will be terrible, horrible day for mankind know the power of God.
* The END DAY will be suffer for bad people, but happiness for who are selected by the angels.

Not many good people at END TIME because they like material world and the Evil more than believe in God:

"As for you, Daniel, keep secret the message and seal the book until the END TIME; many shall fall away and evil shall increase." Daniel 12(4).

The year 2633 is too far for us, but everyone has the END DAY for oneself.

"Therefore, stay awake, for you know neither the day nor the hour." Matthew 24(42), Matthew 25(13), Mark 13(23), Mark 13(37).

Jesus said: "I am the way and the truth and the life. No one comes to Father except through me." John 14(6). Other time Jesus said: "I am the resurrection and the life; whoever believes in me, even if he dies, will live, and everyone who lives and believes in me will never die." John 11(25-26).

Another time Jesus said: "Enter through the narrow gate for the gate is wide and the road broad that leads to destruction, and those who enter through it are many. How narrow the gate and constricted that leads to life. And those who find it are few." Matthew 7(13-14).

The purpose of this book is try to find an answer of the END DAY, so research about God, religions are necessary, not try to disturb anyone or any religion.

Humankind live in a natural world, we are bouncing in ourselves and between Good and Evil, but toward Evil more than Good; Material World and Evil prevent us from God, the Goodness and the Creator.

The END DAY is the death day for mankind. We need to understand each other, and our differences without resulting in conflicts and wars.

WHAT WILL BE HAPPENED
FOR THE EARTH AFTER THE END DAY?

After the END DAY, the world is gone, but the earth and the universe may still remain. God may create a new season and a new harvest.

Perhaps, it needs thousands of years to appear a new kind of people on earth. And some of our astronauts got stuck on Mars or other planets; they lived there and multiply, their descendents change with the environment (small body, big head, big eyes? . . .). When they have a chance to go back the earth, they will become "Ancient U. F. O." for the new mankind? Who know? This process could be happened few times before our ancestors? Just God know, because God can do anything in His will.

REFERENCES

BOOKS:
- The New American Bible (copy right @ 1987 by World Publish, Inc.)
- Complete Guide to the Bible (by Stephen M. Miller. Copy right @ 2007.)
- The Compact Timeline Of The Bible (by Samuel T. Jordan, 2008 by Third Millennium Press Ltd.)
- The Complete Idiot's Guide to Philosophy (Jay Steveson, Ph D. copy right @ 1998 by Alpha Books.)
- The Truth about Muhammad (Robert Spencer copy right 2006.)

INTERNET:
- What is the Galactic Alignment by John Major Jenkins (alignment 2012.com/whatisGA.htm)
- Biography of Philosophers (Wikipedia, the free encyclopedia.)
- Philosophers and religions (Wikipedia, the free encyclopedia.)
- Saint Thomas Aquinas (Wikipedia, the free encyclopedia.)
- History of Hinduism (Wikipedia, the free encyclopedia.)
- History of Buddhism (Wikipedia, the free encyclopedia.)
- Gautama Buddha (Wikipedia, the free encyclopedia.)
- Muhammad (Wikipedia, the free encyclopedia.)
- Muhammad's wives (Wikipedia, the free encyclopedia.)
- The Crusades to the Holy Land (www. Jesuschristsavior.net/crusades.htm/).
- Crusades (Wikipedia, the free encyclopedia.)
- Roman Empires (Wikipedia, the free encyclopedia.)
- Stephen Hawking (Wikipedia, the free encyclopedia.)
- Fatima Network, Our Lady of Fatima on line (fatima.org).
- Mary Faustina Kowalska (Wikipedia, the free encyclopedia.)
- Google Map.

TELEVISION: Science Channel and History Channel:
Big Bang Theory, Black Holes, Wonder of The Universe, the Ancient
U. F. O., Who is God?,
2012 Prophesy.

THE ADDITION PICTURES
ABOUT THE END DAY

(1) The Divine Mercy Image:

In Sunday February 22th, 1931 Jesus appeared to Faustina, a Polish Catholic nun as the "King of Divine mercy" and Jesus told her: "Paint an image according to pattern you see, with the signature: *'Jesus I Trust In You.'* I desire that this image be venerated, first in your chapel, and then through out the world. I promise the soul that will venerate this image will not perish." Sister Faustina was beatified on April 18th,1993 and canonized on April 30th, 2000, the first Saint in the 21st century.

The Divine Mercy is the last chance that Jesus had given to the world in 21st, 22nd, 23rd century. Christian churches are responsible to venerate the Divine Mercy image; many souls will be saved. After the year 2300, Satan will be released, Christians will be suffered and reduced the numbers, Evil and Material World will take control as prophet Daniel had predicted:

> "As for you, Daniel, keep secret the message and seal the book until the END TIME; *many shall fall away and evil shall increase."*
>
> Daniel 12(4)

(2) Diagram of Universes:

* God is the most goodness, the most intelligent and the most fairness. The cause of intelligent has to have a purpose. God's purpose creating angels and mankind to share with Him the Truth, the Goodness and the Beauty. But God also put in them a free will like a program of computer.

* A simple program for a computer is the statement "if and then ..."

    If A = B and then ...

    If A > B and then ...

    If A < B and then ...

For examples:

If John get married with Chris and then his life will be . . . .
If John get married with Tracy and then his life will be . . .
If you smoke and then . . . , if . . . and then . . . , if . . . and then . . . .

* God's program has infinity of "if and then . . ." By "free will" "if and then", it splits to three Universes: God Universe (Heaven), Evil Universe (Hell), and our Natural Universe.

* Our Natural Universe is bouncing between us, God Spirit, and Evil Spirit; one minute we are good, next minute we might turn to bad. By free will, we can choose God, Evil or the world.

* When we die, our bodies remain at the Natural Universe, our souls will pass through the death tunnel and go to a place by judgment of Jesus, the Son of God. Before Jesus time, good souls went to the God Spirit place (Hinduism and Buddhism called Nirvana), and bad souls went to the Evil Spirit place. After Jesus, the Heaven was opened, good souls who follow Jesus will go to Heaven (God Universe). The bad souls who follow Evil will go to Hell (Evil Universe). The souls could not go to Heaven are called death or loss souls.

Jesus I Trust In You

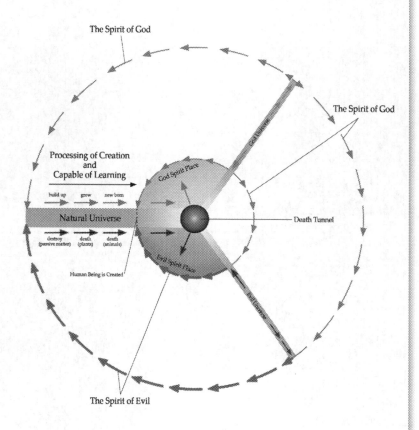

Diagram of Universes

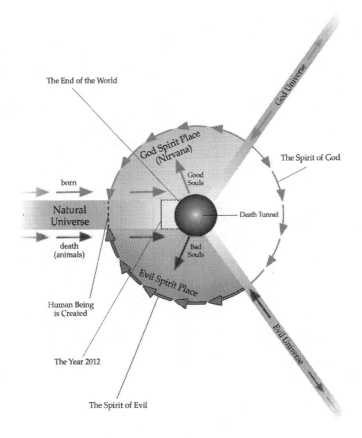

The End of the World

God Universe

God Spirit Place
(Nirvana)

The Spirit of God

born

Good
Souls

Natural
Universe

Death Tunnel

death
(animals)

Bad
Souls

Evil Spirit Place

Human Being
is Created

The Year 2012

Evil Universe

The Spirit of Evil

Diagram of the Place
Where Souls Stay Before
Jesus Christ

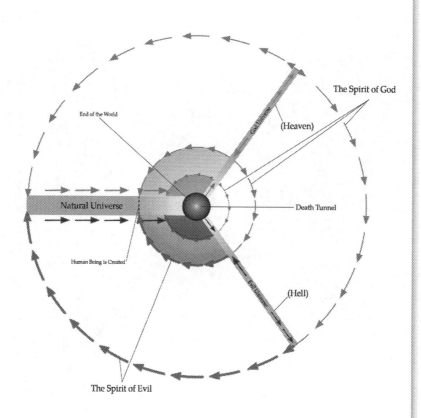

Diagram of the Universe
after Jesus Christ

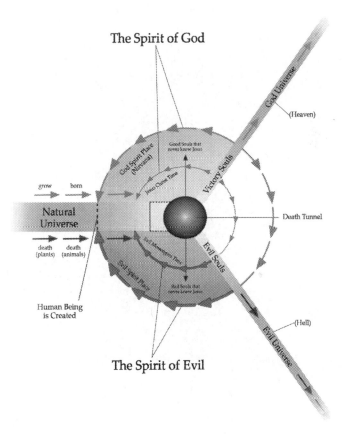

The Spirit of God

Natural Universe

Diagram of the Place
Where Souls Stay After
Jesus Christ

ABOUT THE AUTHOR

Anthony Lenh Dinh Ngo was born on April 30th, 1950 in a village located near the sea of Thai Binh city in North Vietnam. In 1954 when he was 4 years-old, Vietnam became divided. North Vietnam chose to follow Communism, but South Vietnam chose to be a Democratic nation. His parents did not want to live within a Communist nation so they decided to escape to South Vietnam. During this time, the United Nations was evacuating North Vietnamese to South Vietnam. Anyone who wanted to evacuate had to go to Hai Phong city, approximately twenty miles from his village. As a result, Ngo's family chose to travel by boat with a group of other North Vietnamese escapees. On the day of their escape, the men stayed on the boat far from the seashore and from the port to avoid loyal Communist North Vietnamese that would report the escapees to the Communist soldiers. When it was dark, Ngo's mother carried her baby (his sister) and his younger brother, his older sister held his hand; they joined groups with some other women and children and went to the seashore, the place which they had planned. The boat gave off the light signals and the women and children had to walk from the beach into water to reach the boat. They prepared some banana trees for small children can hold on because of deep water; he and his older sister held one banana tree and one lady pushed them. When they came to the boat the water raised up to his mother's nose because of the tide, they could die if they came little later. Fortunately, they sailed to Hai Phong safely and the United Nations flew them to South Vietnam.

After few peaceful years, the war was broken because Communist North Vietnam wanted to occupy South Vietnam. On August 20th, 1970 Ngo joined the South Vietnam Navy and eventually became a Navy Officer. When South Vietnam fell to the North Vietnam on April 30, 1975, he was one of many soldiers placed in "re-education" camps, which were worsen than prisons. He was in the U-Minh forest camp for three years, after which he returned home to his wife and two children. He was tired of living under the harsh Communist government and tired of watching out for local Communist spies. He decided to take his family and attempt to escape Vietnam. However, he had little money and escaping was extremely difficult, but he had a skill that escapees needed, he knew how to drive a boat and navigate the waters. He would try three times before he was successful. The first attempt was made from Ha Tien. Ngo and his family paid for passage, but the boat never arrived. In the second attempt, he drove his friend's boat on the Mekong River, going from Long Xuyen to the sea. But the engine broke down and everyone on the boat was caught by Communist soldiers. The men were taken to prison while the women and children were allowed to return home after one week. The plan for the third attempt also included navigating a boat down the Mekong River from Long Xuyen into the sea. Ngo and a naval friend would be responsible for navigating the boat carrying a group of eighty-three escapees. The group would include his family, two brothers, a sister-in-law, two cousins, and a few friends and their families. The group left on December 15th, 1980. By mid-night they had reached the sea. There was a horrible storm. The little river boat, measuring 39 feet x 9 feet containing a ten horse power engine, was no match against the massive waves of the sea. The waves drenched the boat with water. The only thing they could do was pray. The storm finally passed. After three days at sea, the boat finally landed in Malaysia. The group was sent to a refugee camp on the Malaysian island Paulo Bidong. Ngo, his family, and relatives would spend three months there before the United States approved them as immigrants to the United States. The U.S. then moved them to a refugee camp in Galang II, Indonesia. After two months in Galang II, they were moved to Singapore where they spent one week before being flown to the United States. It was May 21th, 1981.

His life in Vietnam has allowed Ngo to see the conflict between two different ideologies: Communism and Individualism. This conflict has caused a war taking too many lives. A war that has divided families (a war that "dad" and "son" were in different side of the battle, which happened to many Vietnamese families). Now having lived in the United States, a rich, powerful nation with much freedom of choice, he has a better understanding about the world and its conflicts. He is a Catholic because his grandfather was a Buddhist who converted to Catholicism. Many of his cousins, however, continue to be Buddhists. As a result, he enjoys reading and learning about the different world religions and the Bible. His passion for religion has driven him to write this book, to share his insight and discovery from reading and learning about the Bible.